LEADING
AFTER A LAYOFF

LEADING
AFTER A LAYOFF

REIGNITE YOUR TEAM'S
PRODUCTIVITY
IN JUST 12 WEEKS!

RAY SALEMI

New York Chicago San Francisco Lisbon London Madrid Mexico City
Milan New Delhi San Juan Seoul Singapore Sydney Toronto

Library of Congress Cataloging-in-Publication Data

Salemi, Ray.
    Leading after a layoff : reignite your team's productivity in just 12 weeks /
Ray Salemi.
        p.   cm.
     ISBN 978-0-07-163715-2 (alk. paper)
     1. Leadership.   2. Teams in the workplace.   3. Downsizing of
organizations.   4. Layoff systems.   5. Crisis management.   I. Title.

    HD57.7.S245   2010
    658.4'092—dc22   2009016406

Portions of this book were previously published by Adams Media Corporation, 2005.

1 2 3 4 5 6 7 8 9 10 11 12 13 14 15 16 17 18 19 20 21 22   FGR/FGR 0 9

ISBN 978-0-07-163715-2
MHID   0-07-163715-X

Interior design by Think Design Group LLC

McGraw-Hill books are available at special quantity discounts to use as premiums and
sales promotions or for use in corporate training programs. To contact a representative,
please e-mail us at bulksales@mcgraw-hill.com.

For Karen,

whose support, guidance, faith, and love
make all things possible.

CONTENTS

FOREWORD

MY NAME IS Robert G. Allen. In the 1980s, I wrote three best-selling books. Two of them made it to the number one spot on the *New York Times* bestseller list. My first book, *Nothing Down: How to Buy Real Estate with Little or No Money Down*, became the largest-selling, longest-running financial hardcover book in history. My second book, *Creating Wealth*, was also a number one *New York Times* bestseller, with more than a million sold. My next books, *Multiple Streams of Income* and *Multiple Streams of Internet Income*, hit the *New York Times* bestseller list only weeks after they were published. My book *The One Minute Millionaire*, coauthored with Mark Victor Hansen, known as the Chicken Soup for the Soul Guy, hit numerous bestseller lists (including the *New York Times*) within the first few weeks of publication. I have helped thousands of people succeed in business.

As a millionaire maker, I'm often asked for the secret to business success. My advice is simple: find a business system that works and find a mentor to teach it to you. I have successfully mentored thousands of people and taught them the business system that made me successful. Once they mastered the system, they were successful, too. The key is to find a mentor who has succeeded where you want to succeed and who can teach you what to do.

I also tell people that business is full of disasters—especially if people don't have a mentor to help them. There are few business events more dangerous than a layoff. Layoffs can become disasters if they capsize and sink your group. You've lost people, momentum, and perhaps whole pieces of your organization. Your team could flounder for months. When you are struck with a layoff, you need a mentor who has walked the path and can lead you by the hand.

Ray Salemi is the mentor you need to rebuild your team after a layoff. He has more than a decade of experience in leading small teams in companies of all sizes. He has experienced every aspect of layoffs—from being a victim of a layoff to rebuilding teams after corporate downsizing. Experience like this has taught him secrets that you can use as you and your team weather hard times.

It's my firm belief that all the knowledge in the world is useless if you don't know how to put it into action. The world is full of thick business books that teach you tons of theory but never show you what to do. Ray agrees with me that a great management book should show you what to do to succeed and has followed through on his belief. *Leading After a Layoff* is a clear, concise, step-by-step guide that shows you exactly what to do to bring your team back to life.

In case you haven't noticed, layoffs are here to stay. Managers who know how to handle layoffs will ride this wave and have highly successful careers. Managers who don't will be swept into the undertow. Read *Leading After a Layoff* and let Ray show you how to ride the wave.

Preface

I'VE BEEN A frontline manager for more than ten years—the kind of manager who leads teams of individual contributors as they deliver the actual work that makes the company run. I've had more than fifty people work for me in my career, though I've never had a group larger than ten. I've had management jobs in four different companies and led teams in customer support, engineering, and sales. I was fired from my first two management jobs because I was a bad manager, and I did very well at my next two management jobs because I had learned my lessons.

In all that time that I was being a crappy manager and learning the ropes, I discovered two disturbing facts:

1. Being a frontline manager is the toughest job in the company. You are the only manager who leads people whose jobs are significantly different from your own. All higher levels of managers get to lead other managers, but you get to lead customer service agents, product marketing managers, or retail associates.
2. Companies provide very little help to their frontline managers. The CEO and general managers can hire consultants, coaches, and facilitators. If you are lucky, your company will spring for a copy of *The 7 Habits of Highly Effective People*, and if you are very, very lucky, your company will send you to a two-day workshop on frontline management.

I learned these two facts the hard way, by flailing about, trying to become a decent and then a good frontline manager. (I defined *good* as being a manager whom people enjoyed working for and who didn't get himself fired.) In the midst of all that flailing, I learned a few things that I want to pass on. That was the first reason I wrote this book.

The second reason I wrote this book was that I've dealt with many layoffs. I started work in the 1980s when U.S. companies woke up from the pleasant dream of post–World War II dominance (brought on by the fact that the rest of the industrial world had been destroyed) and realized that they had some tough competition out there and that they'd have to start being more flexible about whom they hired and whom they kept. That's when the layoffs started.

I've been through many layoffs. Usually I was unaffected. I've also been laid off four times and had to choose people and lay them off three times. Given the choice between being laid off myself and laying other people off, I'd rather be laid off myself. There's freedom in saying "So long, suckers!" and bolting with your severance package.

I usually survived the layoff, and then I was stuck with fixing a team that had been traumatized by the latest round of corporate cutting and restructuring. I found then that there was no book for frontline managers who were trying to rebuild a team.

There were books such as *Healing the Wounds* by David M. Noer, and they were good for addressing the emotional aspect of layoffs. There were no books, though, for frontline managers who were asking the simple question "What do I do now?" *Leading After a Layoff* answers that question.

I wrote *Leading After a Layoff* so that you would have an action plan. I built this plan based on my experiences as a successful manager and, more important, as a failed manager. I learned a lot more when I was failing than when I was succeeding. The plan takes abstract concepts of leadership, communication, and management and boils them down to action steps. When you follow the action steps, you'll be able to chart your progress in rebuilding your team and making it better than before.

As I write these words, the United States is passing through one of the most difficult economic times in recent memory. Layoffs are rampant, and I hope that this book helps you pass through these times with the confidence not only that you will survive the disruption of a layoff but also that you, and your team, will thrive in our ever-changing economic landscape.

ACKNOWLEDGMENTS

THE NEW AND expanded version of *Leading After a Layoff* exists because of the help of some extraordinary people.

Janet Rosen, my agent from Sheree Bykofsky Associates, was the driving force behind the new edition. Janet's belief in this project, her guidance, drive, and most of all her enthusiasm, made this book a reality. Thank you, Janet!

Chris McGinty, my friend and mentor. Chris's insightful observations about leadership, management, and office politics, usually made over a game of chess, formed the basis for many of the tips in this book. It was common for me to finish a conversation with Chris and run back to my desk to write down his insights before I forgot them. Thank you, Chris, for your guidance and friendship.

I would, again, like to acknowledge the more than fifty people who have worked with me—especially those who worked for me as remote employees and whose only connection to me at many times was an e-mail thread and a phone call. Working with you has made me a better manager and a better person. I believe that you all taught me more than I taught you, and I thank you for your support and companionship.

Introduction

EVERY YEAR, LAYOFFS disrupt the lives of millions of employees. Layoff victims suffer from feelings of abandonment and betrayal. Layoff survivors cope with larger workloads, the loss of their friends, and the uncertainty of their own fates. Meanwhile, the managers left behind must struggle to rebuild teams that have been shattered by the layoff. It is their challenge to help their employees find their footing and begin performing again.

In the mid-1980s, job security was the norm and layoffs were the exception. In the late 1980s, however, new technologies began to destroy companies at a dramatic rate. Globalization removed barriers to foreign competition, and U.S. companies had to become nimble and ready to respond to changes. To survive, companies had to merge, restructure, and cut staff. Today, layoffs have become the norm. Consider Figure 1's chart of layoffs in the United States.

What's amazing about this chart is not that layoffs jumped dramatically in 2001 and again in 2008. What's amazing is that layoffs never really went away. Even the year with the lowest number of layoffs, 2005, still saw more than eight hundred thousand people hit the street.

Layoffs are now a reality of today's business. They are here to stay. They may increase during bad times, but they will not go away during good times. Companies lay people off in bad times because of earnings. They lay them off in good times because of the restructurings and acquisitions that are made possible by a great economy.

Today's highly fluid organizations routinely use reorganizations, reengineering, downsizing, rightsizing, mergers, and acquisitions as tools to enhance shareholder value. There are questions about whether these activities really improve shareholder value in the long run, but these are not the issues you'll face as a frontline manager. You'll need to deal with one employee sobbing in his cubicle while

1

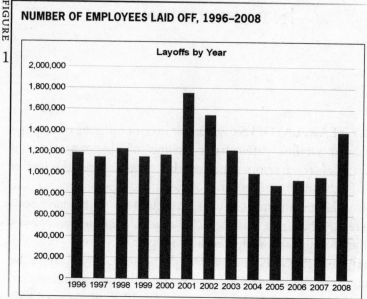

U.S. Department of Labor

another openly polishes her résumé during work hours. You'll have to figure out your group's new mission and show the remaining people how they can get more work done with fewer teammates. To make matters worse, you may have lost your boss, your mentor, or your entire organization. Recovering from a layoff is tough work.

If you are like most managers, you will have had little training in recovering from such a devastating event. Companies train us in how to deliver the bad news without getting sued. They don't teach us how to fix a devastated team.

As a veteran of the high-tech industry, I've seen all sides of layoffs. After more than a decade of experience as a manager, I've discovered the paths that can bring your team back to life after a layoff, and I've discovered ways to make your team less vulnerable to them. *Leading After a Layoff* is a practical, step-by-step plan for refocusing your team. I based the plan on my own experience and the readings I did to become a better manager. Then I distilled all this information into these steps and tips.

There are two aspects to this book. The first is the step-by-step plan with details that explain how to implement these steps with your team. These chapters are information intensive and focus on actions rather than theories. That said, there is enough theory to explain why we're taking the steps.

The second part of the plan is the tips. Management is like golf in that you can know the basics and yet still find some new tip or trick that makes a big difference in your game. I've accumulated these tips over my years in management, and now I'm passing them on to you. You'll see the tips throughout the book.

Leading your team back from a layoff isn't easy, yet it can be done successfully, and you can find the process fulfilling. Our companies implemented the layoffs because difficult times require that all our teams improve their productivity. As a frontline manager, you're part of the management team that delivers that productivity. You'll do that successfully when you follow the steps and tips contained here. The first thing is to make sure you know that the skills you need to succeed as a manager are very different from the ones that you needed to succeed as an individual contributor.

Understanding the Five Key Skills of Management

New managers must understand that management work is nothing like the work their teams do—or, indeed, the work they did just before they became managers. Some managers don't learn this. They believe their job as manager is to be the biggest, fastest, bestest individual contributor in the group. They believe they will lead the group by dint of their tremendous job skills rather than by their tremendous management skills. These managers have a hard life, filled with overwork and management failure.

This is not to say that you should never do the work of your group if you have the skills. You may need to pitch in, especially after a layoff. The key is to remember that you are pitching in and that your individual contribution is something you're doing to help the team, rather than a way to slip into the warm, cozy bed of your comfort zone.

The key to moving away from the world of the individual contributor and toward the life of a manager is to recognize that the skills you need to exhibit as a manager are different from the skills you needed as an individual contributor.

All jobs have five key skills that define great players. These five skills are independent of each other, and sometimes there may be four or six, but five is the usual number. The catch is that these five skills are different for every job. For example, a sales representative has the following five key skills: prospecting, building rapport, listening, translating problems into solutions, and closing business. A salesperson with only four of these five skills is going to have a short, poverty-ridden career.

As managers, we also have five skills that determine our effectiveness. The reason we need to embrace being managers and give up being individual contributors is that we need to be willing to focus on these skills. Figure 2 shows the five skills.

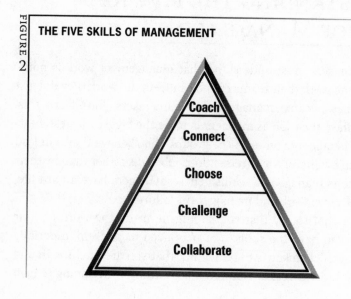

FIGURE 2

THE FIVE SKILLS OF MANAGEMENT

Managers need to excel at these five skills to succeed. The skills build on each other; you need to succeed at the lower skills before you can move up to the next skill in the triangle.

These five skills can also serve as our road map back from a layoff. Following is a summary of each skill. We will look at each of these skills individually, and how to implement them, in the upcoming chapters:

- **Collaborate.** This is the foundation skill. It refers to your ability to create a team of people who trust each other and who take ownership for the team's results. If you've built a foundation of collaboration, your team will feel responsible for the team's goals and you'll help them achieve those goals. This is the basis for all other goals.
- **Challenge.** Teams need to know why they exist and what they are supposed to deliver. These two factors make up the team's challenge. You will help your team uncover its challenge and create goals to achieve it. Your team will buy into a challenge it created in a collaborative effort.
- **Choose.** Once you know what the team is supposed to do, you need to make sure you have the right people to do it. This is where you choose roles for the people on your team and perhaps hire new people for your team. You can't pick the right people until you know what you are going to do, so this step follows the challenge step.
- **Connect.** Together, you and your team must connect the people and goals into a plan. The individuals on your team also need to know how delivering the results will help them achieve their personal goals. This step can be accomplished only after you've got the people and the challenge.
- **Coach.** Once you have the right goals, the right people, and the right plan, you're ready to start coaching. Without these foundations in place you've got nothing specific to use for coaching and you're left giving generic advice such as "Work faster!" This is rarely helpful.

Building a Plan with the Skills

Our layoff recovery plan builds on a framework of the five skills. How long it will take to bring your team back from the layoff depends on the extent of the disruption the layoff caused, which can vary widely from layoff to layoff.

For example, if your team lost only one or two people who, frankly, deserved to be let go, you'll see only minor disruption. In contrast, if two of your management peers were let go along with most of their people, and all the remaining people were combined into one group under you, you are looking at major disruption. In that case you will need to work though all the steps of the plan to turn this collection of people back into a team.

The plan's ultimate goal is to leave you with a team of people who work well together, know what they need to accomplish, and look to you for coaching to improve their skills. The plan lays out a twelve-week program, but you can get through the steps more quickly if your team is in good shape to start with.

Here is a preview of the recovery plan. We'll look at these goals again at each section in the plan and discuss specific steps you can take to achieve these goals.

THE RECOVERY PLAN

DELIVERABLE	DESCRIPTION	DATE
COLLABORATE		
Write a damage report.	Think about your team and answer the questions in Chapter 1 in a report format or in an e-mail to yourself.	Week 1
	Talk to the folks on your team while gathering the data to write this report.	
	Develop a clear understanding of where your team stands today and what needs to be done to rebuild trust.	

DELIVERABLE	DESCRIPTION	DATE
Hold one-on-one meetings with all your team members.	Meet with each of your team members one on one, preferably over lunch or coffee. Listen to how the layoff has affected each person. Take the time to learn about each person's professional and personal goals. Make deposits in the emotional bank account (see Chapter 3) with them.	Week 2
Hold a team meeting to discuss the layoff.	Give your team members a chance to vent their feelings about the layoff. Consider the Quaker meeting format (see Chapter 3) or simply have an informal discussion.	Week 3

CHALLENGE

Have your team present a stakeholder analysis report.	Lead your team through a stakeholder analysis process. Teach your team about the four stakeholders and how to discover what each stakeholder wants from your team (see Chapter 5). Show the analysis to your stakeholders and get their agreement.	Week 4
Publish a mission statement.	Lead your team through the mission-creation process (see Chapter 6). Have a training meeting, perhaps with another manager, to start the process. Help the team discuss the mission; lead the team through the mission-crafting process.	Week 5
Publish goals.	Help your team translate the mission and stakeholder analysis into SMART goals (see Chapter 7).	Week 6
Publish roles for your team.	Create a work flow for your team and define the roles and job descriptions that will make your team run smoothly. Share your ideas with the team and get feedback; then deliver the final role descriptions to your team.	Week 7

DELIVERABLE	DESCRIPTION	DATE
CHOOSE		
Assign people to roles.	Find the best matches between your team members and the available roles (see Chapter 9). Work with team members to assign roles that suit them.	Week 8
Publish a team plan.	Work with the team to define the projects, tasks, and feedback system that will implement the team's goals (see Chapter 10).	Week 9
CONNECT		
Hold three feedback sessions.	Create a tradition of execution by taking constant feedback about the tasks and helping the team devise new plans to achieve the goals.	Weeks 10, 11, 12
Create win-win agreements.	Help team members find their internal motivation for fulfilling their role and make an explicit agreement with each person to help the person achieve personal goals from work.	Week 11
COACH		
Create coaching agreements with all willing team members.	Create coaching agreements so each of your people will have a clear development goal.	Week 12
Find a coaching moment.	Find an opportunity to coach your team members on a skill chosen in the coaching agreement.	Week 12
Deliver coaching feedback.	Deliver feedback to your employees to help them see behaviors and devise an improvement plan.	Week 12

At the end of this development plan, you will have taken a group that may have been in complete disarray and moved it toward becoming a high-functioning team. This is not an easy job, and pulling it off will make you one of the best managers in your company.

PART 1

REBUILDING TRUST
AND THE SPIRIT OF
COLLABORATION

The first step is to rebuild trust and collaboration on your team. This is not a process that happens quickly; it will take at least three weeks before it becomes an ongoing part of the way you manage.

Following is a table of specific measurable goals you can accomplish in the next three weeks. I've designed these goals so that you will know whether you've accomplished them. There is no way to fudge whether you've written a damage report and e-mailed it to yourself, or had one-on-one meetings with your team members, or held a group meeting to discuss the layoff.

Each of these deliverables is due on the Friday of the week in question. You decide which Friday marks the end of Week 1. You can also bring these goals in faster; for example, you may decide that you want to have your team meeting before you hold one-on-one meetings. That's fine as well.

Your goals for the first three weeks are shown here.

COLLABORATE

DELIVERABLE	DESCRIPTION	DATE
Write a damage report.	Think about your team and answer the questions in Chapter 1 in a report format or in an e-mail to yourself.	Week 1
	Talk to the folks on your team while gathering the data to write this report.	
	Develop a clear understanding of where your team stands today and what needs to be done to rebuild trust.	
Hold one-on-one meetings with all your team members.	Meet with each of your team members one on one, preferably over lunch or coffee. Listen to how the layoff has affected each person.	Week 2
	Take the time to learn about each person's professional and personal goals. Make deposits in the emotional bank account (see Chapter 3) with them.	

DELIVERABLE	DESCRIPTION	DATE
Hold a team meeting to discuss the layoff.	Give your team members a chance to vent their feelings about the layoff. Consider the Quaker meeting format (see Chapter 3) or simply have an informal discussion.	Week 3

Collaboration is the foundation of all great team performance. It speaks to an environment where everybody on the team understands the team's goals and is invested in their delivery. It describes an environment of trust, where team members work together to see all sides of a problem and develop the best solution.

Collaboration is the best way for teams to work together, but it is not the natural way that teams work together. When people work instinctively (without thinking about it), we get something very different from collaboration. We get teams where the manager feels personal responsibility for the team's success and the happiness of its members and where team members feel disconnected from an outcome they cannot control.

Teams led by instinct tend to form cliques that battle for scraps of resources and recognition given out by a central and powerful leader. They tend to form environments where the team members don't trust each other and worry that someone else on the team is getting too big a piece of the pie.

Left to their own devices, teams lack trust. The members don't trust the leader, don't trust each other, and don't trust the team as an entity that will get the job done. As a result, they waste hours battling over the insignificant and pointing fingers while their customers' cries for help get ignored.

This situation is especially common just after a layoff, when everyone on the team has seen what happens to people who let themselves be labeled expendable. The knives were out just before the layoff, and nobody is sure that they should be put away yet. Résumés are polished, people have one foot out the door, and everybody is waiting for the other shoe to drop.

This is where you start after a very bad layoff. Your situation may be better—you may work for a company or in an industry where layoffs are common. Everyone may agree with the choices, and they may just shrug their shoulders, count who's left, and go back to work. Even so, trust may have been shattered, and if trust has been broken it's your job to repair it.

This is why *collaborate* is the foundation management skill. Great managers build trust and create teams where people are eager to work together. They consciously examine the state of their teams and themselves and make a plan to bring the team back to the point where everybody is connected to a common goal.

In the Introduction, you learned what the five key skills of management are. The four chapters that follow will show you exactly what to do to understand the situation ahead of you, to build an environment where people take ownership of the team's deliverables, and to help your teams move beyond the baggage of a layoff.

Those four chapters cover the first steps of your rebuilding:

✦ Surveying the damage
✦ Leading so others will follow
✦ Fostering emotional recovery
✦ Collaborating with remote employees

These steps are the crucial foundation of the team we are building. Let's get started.

SURVEYING THE
DAMAGE

BEFORE YOU CAN fix something, you need to know where it's broken. Teams can be broken in many ways. People may have lost faith in the company, themselves, or their work. Trust is the basis of great teamwork, and it is the first thing that gets damaged or destroyed in a layoff.

In addition to lost trust, your team may be suffering from a variety of emotional syndromes, including survivor's guilt, anger, or depression. What's worse, the team may not be acknowledging any of these, and instead of open emotional displays you'll see backbiting, bickering, and plummeting work performance.

There are more mundane problems as well. Your team may have relied on people who are no longer there—particularly if the layoff merges departments or reorganizes teams under a new manager. Your team may feel the need to compete against each other or against other groups.

Finally, if your department has been merged, you'll find that trust and teamwork are difficult for the simple fact that the people don't know each other.

There are two aspects to being a manager. One is management, where you figure out how to best utilize resources. The

15

other aspect is leadership, where you help people work through change. Rebuilding trust is a leadership task.

It's your job to guide your team past this difficult time and back to a place of performance. Once you have used your leadership skills to reestablish a sense of shared vision for your team, you'll be able to use your management skills to reorganize your team to meet its new challenges. The first two steps of the rebuilding process—collaborate and challenge—focus on leadership instead of management.

The question is, where is your team? Are team members angry? Are they depressed? Perhaps they don't care about the layoff. I've worked for companies that have had so many layoffs that people treat them the way people in Boston treat a snowstorm: they complain, they take a day off, and then they shovel the walk, brush off the car, and go back to work.

We think by asking questions. Questions direct our attention and allow us to see what's going on around us. This step presents questions you should ask yourself and your team after a layoff. Working through these questions brings to the surface the issues affecting your team so you'll know what needs to be done to rebuild trust.

There are two things you need to do right after a layoff:

+ Assess yourself
+ Assess the team

Doing an assessment sounds like a big job, but it is nothing more than answering a list of questions. Your first goal during this first step is to write a report on the status of you and your team by answering the questions in this chapter.

First, Assess Yourself

Jack Welch, the legendary CEO of General Electric, once said that you shouldn't be a manager if you couldn't lay people off and that you shouldn't be a manager if laying people off didn't bother you.

Layoffs are emotional and difficult. Good managers feel bad about layoffs. Great managers are honest about how the layoff has affected them emotionally and take care of themselves.

Anyone who has flown on an airplane has learned the cardinal rule of airline safety: "Make sure your oxygen mask is in place before you help others." This is a commonsense practice that people forget in stressful situations. Most parents would instinctively put on their child's mask before their own, forgetting that an unconscious parent can't help a child.

We managers tend to ignore this rule when it comes to recovering from a layoff. We worry about "our people" and believe that we need to be strong "for the team." Though we are grieving, we deny it.

Before we can assess the state of the group, we need to understand how we feel. Some of us quickly process the emotions that follow a layoff; others get stuck in feelings of sadness or guilt.

The first step is acknowledging the effect the layoff had on you. People in business situations tend to deny feelings of loss. Managers are especially susceptible to this reflex. Unfortunately, if you feel you cannot show your pain, your team will follow suit.

One incident that I remember illustrates how we ignore feelings. I worked for a sales team that had to change office buildings because the landlord wanted to rent our office space to a growing dot-com. We had been in that office for more than eighteen years and had grown accustomed to how the building worked. We had a nice kitchen, underground parking, and a recreation room with a big-screen television and a Ping-Pong table. We were happy.

As moving day approached, we began to clean out our cubes. Signs that said "Liquidate" appeared on our furniture. We used gallows humor to feel better about our loss, joking that perhaps signs saying "Terminate" should go on our nameplates.

The day I packed up and emptied my cube was very emotional. I didn't understand why until I remembered that I had been laid off four times in my career and I had associated the action of packing up my cube with being let go. Once I realized that, I told a few people about my feelings and felt better.

At the end of that last day, we were sitting in someone's office drinking a farewell scotch when I said, "I feel sad about leaving." At that point other guys said, "Yeah—I feel sad too," and "You know, I've been in this place for eighteen years—longer than all of you." Until that point none of us had expressed our feelings of loss over something as simple as switching office space. Imagine the emotions that get stifled over a traumatic layoff.

Your employees do not need an example of stony resolve to work through the disruption of a layoff. They need someone to show them how to discuss the pain and work through it. You can help them work through their issues only if you do it first. You need to be their example.

Coming to terms with a layoff is a matter of self-reflection, and self-reflection is mostly a matter of asking ourselves questions. Most thinking consists of asking ourselves questions and providing answers (notice this in yourself the next time you are working through a problem). The key to successful self-reflection is asking the right questions. Here are some good ones to consider after a layoff.

Did I Lay Off My Friends?

You worked closely with your ex-employees. You coached them. You mentored them. You saw them every day, may have spent more time with them than with your spouse, and met their families. You socialized with them. You did all those things because you liked them and you wanted to work well together. Now they are gone, and it is natural to miss them.

What's worse, they may be gone because you decided that they were the weakest people on your team. You decided it, and you let your friends go in the layoff. It's hard to get through that process without feeling that perhaps you betrayed their trust. I know that this feeling has hit me every time I've laid people off; it's the reason I'd rather be laid off myself than lay others off.

Have I Lost Friends Among My Peers?

The same loss occurs with your peers. Managers have a tough job, and if they are doing their job right, they've developed relationships with their peers to compare notes and help each other achieve the department's goals.

You and your management peers have attended team meetings, had meals, and worked through difficult management issues. Peers you work with for many years become friends. Now they're gone. It's important to acknowledge that loss so you can come to grips with it.

Have I Lost a Comfortable Situation?

You may have developed a comfortable flow of work with your team. It may have taken months, or even years, to assemble and train the right team of people. Having all of this disrupted is frustrating, and it is OK to be angry about starting over. Does this bother you?

Have I Lost My Sense of Security?

Today most people know there is no job security. Still, we like to believe this is true only for other people and other organizations. Having a layoff hit so close to home shatters your sense of having found a safe place. Do you feel that you've lost your feeling of job security? Is this bothering you?

Have I Lost Confidence in My Company?

It's good to feel connected to a winning team. Losing confidence in your company destroys those good feelings. It's important to recognize this loss and focus on rebuilding that confidence. Leading a team is difficult enough without trying to lead one when you've given up on the company.

Take some time to consider these areas of loss and how they may have affected you. Many companies have an employee assistance program to help employees work through emotional issues. Read books, such as *Healing the Downsized Organization: What Every Employee Needs to Know About Today's New Workplace*, by Delorese Ambrose, or *Healing the Wounds: Overcoming the Trauma of Layoffs and Revitalizing Downsized Organizations* by David Noer,

BE PROUD OF YOUR COMPANY

It is easy, especially after a layoff, to become cynical about your company. Obviously, things aren't going well. People are depressed. The economy is in the tank. It's easy to be cynical—but leave that for other people.

Nobody wants to work for a cynical manager. Instead, find a way to be proud of your company and what you do. Be proud of the way the company handled the layoffs, or proud of the way it is moving forward, or proud of the products, or even proud of your customers. Imbue what you and your team do every day with some meaning.

Notice that I'm not saying "Act proud" or "Pretend to be proud." I'm saying *be* proud. Find something in your company that you can be proud of and stick to that. People can smell deception, and the last thing they need is a manager who is not genuine.

Being proud of your company doesn't mean you need to take a Pollyanna attitude. It doesn't mean that you stick your fingers in your ears, close your eyes, and say, "There are no layoffs. There are no layoffs." It doesn't mean disconnecting yourself from reality. It means focusing your attention where it will do the most good.

We see what we focus on. If we look for instances of the company's screwing up, we will find them. If we look for instances of the company's doing the right thing, we will find those too. If we're focusing our attention on the positive, it will rub off on our team and they will start to focus on the positive as well.

Be warned: you will be challenged if you adopt a positive attitude about the company during dark times. It's easy to be negative, and you'll have team members who will take the easy path. Let them. Remember that there are people on your team who secretly want to be positive but who don't want to put themselves out there. Give them an example of hope and you'll find that their voices will grow stronger with time.

---

about how other companies have worked through layoffs. These books will help you compare your experience to that of other managers in similar situations and also learn from their experiences.

NEXT, ASSESS THE TEAM

Different teams respond to layoffs differently. Some teams will be devastated by a layoff and will exhibit what consultant David Noer, in *Healing the Wounds,* calls "layoff survivor sickness": "It begins with a deep sense of violation. It often ends with angry, sad, and depressed employees, consumed with their attempt to hold on to jobs that have become devoid of joy, spontaneity, and personal relevancy."

This is a sad and depressing situation. But not all teams react this way. Many people just look at each other, shrug, and go back to work. While they may feel some sadness for the coworkers whose lives have been disrupted, they don't feel the sense of violation and alienation that can cripple a team after a layoff.

Three key factors determine why some teams are traumatized by a layoff while others take it in stride:

- ← Emotional dependence
- ← Fairness
- ← Insecurity

Once you understand these influences, you'll know whether your team is likely to have a significant emotional reaction to the layoff. What is more important, you'll understand whether your team's members will feel that their trust in you has been ruptured by the layoffs. As you have your one-on-one meetings, keep the following questions in mind. Later, write the answers in a notebook or note them in an e-mail to yourself. Writing the answers forces us to think about them and cements them in our minds.

Are Your Team Members Emotionally Dependent on the Organization?

Until the 1980s there was an unspoken contract between large companies and employees. The companies promised that employees who did their jobs and were good corporate citizens would always have work. The employees promised to be loyal to the company. Because of that contract, people allowed themselves to become emotionally dependent on the companies. Their coworkers became their family.

Today, this contract is dead. Almost everyone has been laid off at least once or has been involved in a company that has gone through downsizing. Smart employees have begun to think of themselves as independent contractors—even if they have a traditional job. When layoffs hit, the emotional damage is limited because these people have not allowed themselves to become emotionally dependent on their company.

Ask yourself how your team members view their relationship to the company. Did they buy into an unwritten contract of security, or did they understand that all jobs are transient? Does your team feel betrayed by the layoffs, or were the members simply saddened by the necessities of business? Answering these questions will give you a clue to your team's emotional state.

Are Your Team Members Interdependent?

You need to understand how much collaboration your team needs to succeed. Different kinds of teams need different levels of teamwork. A baseball team is a collection of independent individuals who work together—each player bats alone and fields his position alone. A football team, on the other hand, is interdependent—the plays are tightly integrated. How interdependent is your team?

It is easier to reestablish collaboration when team members are independent. A team of loose collaborators will recover quickly if some of them leave the group. If your team members are highly interdependent, however, you'll be rebuilding entire work flows, and you'll need strong collaboration to move forward. Being aware of the level of interdependence among your team members will help you understand the effect the layoff has on their ability to do their job.

Does Your Team Feel That You and the Company Acted Fairly?

Employees continue to trust a company if they believe that the choices about how employees were let go were understandable and fair. Seniority-based layoffs are the classic example of this fairness concept. People may disagree about the number of people who needed to be cut, but the reasons those people were chosen are clear to everyone: seniority ruled.

Employees will see performance-based layoffs as fair if the expectations regarding performance were made explicit and the measures for evaluating each employee's performance were clear and free of bias. Schedules for engineers, quotas for salespeople, and closed-service requests for customer-support organizations all represent clear and unbiased performance measures. If employees believe the people who were let go were underachievers ("deadwood"), a layoff may even improve morale.

There are times when the company's changing needs require it to lay off good employees. For example, companies naturally move from selling individual products to selling complete solutions. This shift requires a new set of skills that cannot be taught quickly. The business may choose to replace currently successful salespeople with those who already possess the required abilities.

Employees see these layoffs in a better light if the new requirements are defined prior to the layoff. If the requirements changed as part of a restructuring process, then the new requirements need to be defined for the team as soon as possible so team members can understand the logic of the choices.

The worst choices are those that surprise the team and seem politically motivated. The most obvious situation is where the person let go was a good performer but had personality conflicts with management. Wise employees may simply nod their heads and say, "Well, that's what happens when you poke the bear," yet even they will chafe (privately) against the perceived unfairness of the decision—and they will not trust the manager who made such a decision.

Surprises damage trust, and perceived favoritism damages trust. If either of these happened in your layoff, you should be prepared for the process of rebuilding that trust to be long.

Who Made the Layoff Choices?

Your first job is to rebuild trust between you and your team. This task is easier if you are not the person who picked the team members who were laid off. If you were handed a list of names, your

TREAT DIFFERENT PEOPLE DIFFERENTLY

There is a myth in management that we must treat all our employees the same way so that we will "be fair." This is a mistake for the simple reason that people don't want to be treated the same way. This is especially true of the high-performing people we want on our teams. Geniuses may have ten times the productivity of average employees, but they can also be particular and persnickety. It's the price they pay for focusing on their craft.

Therefore, if you want to have a high-performing team of people who will deliver ten times the productivity of the average worker, you need to be flexible and creative. This is your side of the productivity bargain.

For example, I know a manager who had an outstanding sales engineer on his team. This guy could make the software sing and make our biggest customers very happy. He worked as many hours as it took, traveled as much as was needed, and delivered results completely, accurately, and quickly. He was also terrible at filling out expense reports.

When the accounting team began to send threatening e-mails to this sales engineer, the manager intervened. The manager knew that there was no way this sales engineer would become good at expense reports, so he asked the group's administrative assistant to fill out the sales engineer's expense reports—he would only have to sign them.

This is a great example of inserting flexibility into a corporate structure to let your geniuses thrive. The corporate policy required that expense reports be filled out promptly. This employee wasn't good at that part of the job, and the manager responded with creativity.

Corporate policies are the enemy of greatness. In an effort to avoid the slightest hint of unfairness, they create a structure of regulations that stifle greatness in service of equality. As a manager of geniuses, you need to be willing to bend the rules and help your team members focus on their strengths.

This is not to say that geniuses get a free ride for every social dysfunction they'd like to inflict on the team. Some of them can be obnoxious; some don't shower; some openly insult their coworkers. If they are creating an atmosphere where they are poisoning the team, or obviously hurting others, you must step in.

Your job, as a manager, is to create an environment where people can flourish. Your greatest creativity shines through when you hire a genius and find a way to let that genius focus on delivering great results.

team members are likely to band together with you in their worries about upper management.

Who made the layoff decisions is less important if employees feel that the layoffs were fair or understandable. However, if they seem arbitrary or politically motivated, the question of who made those choices is critical.

At this point we are just assessing the damage by asking questions. Did you choose the people who were let go? Do you think your employees trust you less because of it?

Do the Team Members Feel the Need to Compete Against Each Other?

When we're preparing for a layoff, we create a prioritized list of employees. The lowest-ranked employees are the ones who are let go.

This prioritization is a reality of business; even so, comparing employees makes teamwork difficult. Teammates who feel they must compete for jobs are more likely to withhold help and to disengage from the group. You need to understand how competitive your employees feel toward each other.

Once you've looked at these questions, you'll have a clear idea of the state of your team. Are your team members ready to trust you, each other, and the company enough to be forthcoming in their work environment?

WRITE YOUR REPORT

Write a report containing your assessment of your team's trust. You don't need to share this report. You are writing it so that you have a measurable deliverable to tell yourself you did a proper analysis of the situation.

You can write the report and leave it on your hard drive, you can share it with your manager, or you can just e-mail it to yourself and forget about it. You probably won't need to read it again since the value lies in writing it.

We've talked a lot about trust because trust is the foundation of high-performing teams. When employees open up and share ideas freely, they become vulnerable. People will allow themselves to become vulnerable only in a trusting environment. You need to determine the state of your team and how ready the team members are to move on to the next steps.

If trust has been damaged severely, you should expect the rebuilding process to be much slower. People will not share their

FOCUS ON THINGS YOU CAN CONTROL

You can't control the fact that there was a layoff. You can't control the economy. You can't control the weather. You can't control the fact that recent cost-cutting measures reduced your team's vacation. You can't control a lot more than you can control.

Yet you can control your attitude. You can control how you interview people. You can control what you say. You can control whether you press reply-to-all on the e-mail when you're angry. You can control how you give advice and whether you give feedback. You can control whether your team has a plan and whether that plan is defined clearly.

You have a choice about where you focus your attention. You can focus on the things you can't control, or you can focus on the things you can control. You control your focus with your thoughts.

Think about your plan. Think about your team. Think about whom you're going to hire and how you're going to coach them. Think about your deadlines. Think about the attitude you are transmitting to your team. Think about collaborating, challenging, choosing, connecting, and coaching.

The things that we think about take over our minds. If we think about the things we can't control, we feel helpless and unhappy. Then we transmit depression to our team. If we think about the things we can control, we feel empowered and optimistic. Then we transmit optimism to our team.

Focus on what you can control and be happier.

---

feelings and thoughts in an unsafe environment. This will slow your team's ability to work together and make it difficult for them to assume the additional responsibilities you'll need them to take on. You'll need to be patient in these cases and work on building your emotional bank account with the team members. Once you've rebuilt trust, you'll be able to move the team forward.

LEADING SO OTHERS WILL FOLLOW

TO REBUILD YOUR team after a layoff, you must master two critical skills: managing and leading. Management is about using scarce resources to maximum effect. It is about planning, guidance, and feedback. Leadership is about helping your team negotiate times of change. Leaders hold the vision of what the team can be in the future and help the team see it. Leaders see where things are today and where they could be in the future and feel compelled to bridge the gap. Leadership is what you need to lay a new foundation for your team.

Leadership is a largely misunderstood practice. Most managers don't have a clear idea of what it means to be a leader or how to inspire a team to achieve more than it thinks is possible. Much of the misunderstanding about leadership comes from our popular image of leaders. When most of us think about leadership, we think of Hollywood creations like Captain Kirk from the original "Star Trek" series.

Captain Kirk was the epitome of the heroic leader. He sat in his big chair on the bridge while his crew fed him information, waiting for Kirk, the hero, to come up with the plan that would save the day.

Heroic leaders look good on television. Who wouldn't want to be seen as Captain Kirk, delivering guidance, courage, and the plan that saves the day? But how would Kirk fare in a conference room facing a team of employees trying to reorganize after a layoff?

Most managers, unfortunately, try to live this fantasy. The typical staff meeting has the leader sitting at the head of a conference table while team members report information. The leader collects input from the team members, stuffs it all into—one hopes—an enormous brain, and hands down wise decisions.

Though this is the most common form of leadership, it is not the most effective. It works poorly in today's dynamic, highly complex business environment. The problems of a layoff cannot be solved with heroic leadership. Effective leaders give up the central role most people expect them to take. They delegate responsibility and trust the team (including themselves as team members) to come up with the best solution. They deflect praise and attention from themselves and give ownership of their projects away. This is not the Hollywood mode of leadership, but it is the most effective one.

In his book *Outliers*, Malcolm Gladwell showed that heroic leadership can be downright dangerous. He discusses airline crashes that occurred on jets that were functioning perfectly but that crashed due to the crew's showing so much deference to their heroic leader, the pilot, that they did not make themselves clear.

One of the most poignant stories involved an Air Florida first officer from a 1982 crash who hinted three times that the wings were covered in ice. But he was so circumspect that the captain never heard him. In another case a particularly deferential crew allowed the plane to run out of fuel rather than make their situation clear to either the captain or the air traffic controller.

Flying an airliner is a complex task that requires a team's cooperation; so is creating an outstanding customer service experience or delivering a new product to the market. All these tasks require more information than a single person can absorb and process. This is why they require us to build a team of committed people rather than try to be the hero.

The best leaders avoid the limelight. Heroic leadership doesn't work, because people don't want to feel like pawns in someone else's grand plan. People who feel like owners will give their best. People who feel like appendages will do the minimum.

Sam Palmisano, the man who replaced Lou Gerstner as CEO of IBM, demonstrated shared leadership. The first thing Palmisano did was ask the board to cut his bonus in half and set it aside as incentive money for his team of top executives. This move cost Palmisano somewhere between $3 million and $5 million of personal income. He explained it by saying, "If you say you're about a team, you have to be a team. You've got to walk the talk, right?"

Palmisano understood that while heroic leadership may be common, it is not effective. Let's take a moment to understand heroic leadership and compare it to the kind of shared leadership that builds strong teams.

Common Leadership Mistakes

Heroic leadership interferes with collaboration, so you need to be able to recognize it in yourself and others. Once you can see it, you can take steps to move beyond it. Here is my definition of heroic leadership: The leader assumes total responsibility for delivering the results. The team members assume responsibility for delivering their part to the leader.

At first glance this definition looks like common sense. We hire managers to deliver results, and they then hire people to do the work. However, this model for looking at the world is outdated relative to modern business. To see why, consider its source.

The modern hierarchical business organization was created by Harrington Emerson (1853–1931), a great management consultant during the Industrial Revolution. Emerson was there when Prussian field marshal Helmuth von Moltke defeated Napoleon III's armies in 1870—then considered among the best in the world. Emerson decided that the Prussian army's tactical advantage was its line and staff management structure. In this structure, line officers did the fighting, while staff officers did the strategic thinking. The staff officers assumed responsibility for victory or defeat, while the line officers were responsible for their piece of the battle. It was a powerful organizational structure for the urgencies of war.

When the Industrial Revolution hit its stride around the turn of the twentieth century and entrepreneurs began creating the largest business organizations in history, Emerson suggested using the Prussian army's line and staff method as a model for large companies. Business leaders and companies such as General Motors took his advice.

The heroic model of management (also known as *command and control*) was the perfect prescription for the assembly-line businesses of the turn of the century. There were no real teams in these businesses. Employees on the assembly line were interchangeable and easily replaceable, and managers treated them as such.

While these war-based techniques were successful for managing assembly-line workers, they are ineffective in today's dynamic, team-oriented businesses. Consider some of the differences between the assembly-line group and a team of knowledge workers—for example, customer-service engineers.

	EARLY ASSEMBLY-LINE WORKERS	CUSTOMER-SERVICE ENGINEERS
Employees	Uneducated, easily replaced	Highly educated, difficult to replace
Tasks	Repetitive physical activity	Complex technical interactions
Exposure to customers	None	Responsible for company image
Teamwork	None needed	Information sharing and handling of customer issues
Organization	Unchanging	Dynamic

The heroic leadership style is no longer suitable in today's business environments. The Prussians' set-piece battles were static and could be understood by a single person. The more efficient army would win. Business in the early 1900s was the same way. Since markets changed slowly, companies could focus on being efficient rather than flexible.

Today flexibility supersedes efficiency. Centralized, highly efficient companies often do the wrong thing, while flexible companies can respond to the marketplace more quickly. A heroic management style is good for efficiency but not for flexibility.

The workforce has also changed considerably since the early 1900s. The uneducated factory workers who ran the assembly lines were, like soldiers, willing to take orders and do what they were told. Early assembly-line workers had specific physical tasks that they could carry out whether or not they were excited by the job.

Today's college-educated knowledge workers want to be part of the decision-making process. Knowledge workers need energy and motivation to carry out their complicated, thought-based tasks. It may be possible to order someone to turn a screw and get results regardless of that person's motivation or morale. However, this is not the case with knowledge workers: you cannot order an unmotivated person to create an inspired marketing campaign or innovative product.

Before you count on collaboration to help you rebuild your team, you need to determine whether you are using the heroic leadership style. Here are some questions that can help.

Do You Put Complete Responsibility for Results on Your Own Shoulders?

Heroic managers see themselves as the only person responsible for delivering the team's results. To a degree, this makes sense. Your boss and your peers cannot communicate with a team of people; they need a point person, and as manager that is your job. Thus, your boss and peers measure you by your team's ability to deliver.

However, some managers take their role as a point person and distort it. They take the responsibility for overall results away from the team and put it on their own shoulders. A perfect example of this is a manager who tries to motivate her team by telling them that if they don't make their numbers she will be fired. Though the manager is holding the team members responsible for their deliverables, she is assuming the entire responsibility for the team's meeting or not meeting its performance goals.

Do You Make All Team-Related Decisions?

Heroic managers usually make all the decisions for the team. They gather input from their team members, take it under advisement, and then deliver a decision. This causes members of the team to become lobbyists instead of partners in the decision-making process. They learn that the only way to have an impact is to influence the heroic manager; they therefore focus on their influencing skills rather than on the problem at hand.

Do You Give Rewards and Punishment?

Heroic managers tend to think of themselves as parents rather than as business partners with their employees. They look for opportunities to praise individuals who do the right thing, and they punish those who do the wrong thing.

Heroic managers use a variety of tools to distribute rewards and punishments. Rewards may be bonuses, praise in front of the group, extra days of vacation, or good reviews. Punishments may be verbal scolding, embarrassment in front of peers, or bad reviews. This causes the employees to act like children rather than mature businesspeople. Desperate to preserve their job security, employees will compete for validation from the manager and point the finger at other coworkers to avoid slaps on the wrist.

Do You Try to Sell Decisions?

Since heroic managers make decisions without team input, they have to sell their decisions to their staff. Some managers treat their own team as they would a customer account or outside client. They pitch their ideas to the most outspoken or influential members first. They try to marginalize those who are likely to disagree. In some cases they simply pull rank and tell the team how things will happen.

Managers who are consistently selling their decisions to their team have probably severed the team relationship. In fact, in cases like this it is more than likely that the team will band together and work against, rather than with, the manager. This can turn ugly. I once worked for an engineering company where a manager wanted to implement software code reviews to avoid errors. Though the idea had merit, the manager rammed the idea down his team's throat. He required formal reviews for insignificant modifications. The team revolted. Mild-mannered software engineers turned into crusaders who wanted the manager fired. The team mocked the manager and held secret meetings to plot against him. In the end, HR had to intervene.

Do You Feel Personally Responsible for Employees?

Heroic leaders often try to live up to their image by assuming personal responsibility for their employees. Employees become willing accomplices in this behavior when they believe their manager should take responsibility for their careers and their happiness. Managers who do this suffer from stress because they are taking on responsibility for things they cannot control.

I knew one manager who was assigned to an overworked customer-service organization. At his first meeting his employees vented that they were overworked and hated their jobs. Rather than work with his team to solve the problem, this manager made it his personal responsibility to fix the lives of his employees. Eventually this led to sleepless nights, chest pains, and continuous stress. He had let them hand him their problems and make him responsible for fixing their lives. It was a disaster.

While this is an unhealthy situation in normal times, it is completely debilitating during a layoff. Managers who feel personally responsible for their employees' happiness during a layoff cannot win. Employees are not going to be happy during layoffs. Period.

This example demonstrates another face of the heroic style. It's easy to see that an overbearing, controlling manager is using the heroic style. It's harder to see that a nice, empathic manager is doing the same thing. Heroic management is not a question of a manager's niceness. It is a question of whether the manager is taking personal responsibility for everything rather than sharing the responsibility with the team.

Do You Act As an Intercom Between Your Team and Upper Management?

It's ironic, but heroic managers will lose their autonomy due to their need to take on all responsibilities. They view themselves as personally responsible for the team's mission and role in the company, so they often become upper management's mouthpiece to the team. Yet they also view themselves as personally responsible for the well-being of their employees, so they become the team's mouthpiece to upper management.

Managers who have made this mistake get torn apart by the conflicting needs of their upper-management team and their employees. They have taken on so many different responsibilities from so many different parties that they can no longer take independent action.

We've seen that heroic leadership happens when the leader takes personal responsibility for the team's mission and the people on the team, rather than working in partnership with them. We've looked at some behaviors that define heroic leadership. Now let's look at the consequences of heroic leadership.

The Costs of the Wrong Leadership Style

The "Star Trek" episode "Tomorrow Is Yesterday" provides my favorite example of the costs of heroic leadership. In this episode, the *Enterprise* has been thrown back in time to 1960s Earth, where it is spotted flying over the United States. The United States launches a jet fighter to investigate the UFO, and Kirk tries to keep the plane at bay with the tractor beam. Well, the plane is crushed and Kirk is forced to beam the pilot to the *Enterprise.*

Our hero, Kirk, runs down to the transporter room and has a long introductory conversation with the pilot. He turns to go when he is interrupted by the intercom. It is Spock, who asks if it is OK for them to turn off the tractor beam.

I keep waiting for Kirk to say, "Well, I don't know, Spock. You're supposed to be so smart, what do you think? Can't you people do any of your own thinking?" But instead, Kirk gives the OK to this trivial task.

This "Star Trek" moment illustrates the most insidious problem with heroic leadership: its tendency to destroy a team's willingness to take the initiative. This happens because heroic leadership creates an environment where it makes more sense for employees to compete than to collaborate. When you are working for a heroic manager, there is a certain mind-set that maximizes your chances for success. Heroic managers cause their employees to think like this:

- **I'm responsible only for my job.** Since my boss has taken responsibility for the total deliverable, it makes the most sense for me to focus exclusively on my role on the team. I won't get credit for the leader's results, only my own, so why do more than the minimum?
- **It's most important to make my boss happy.** Since my boss is handing out the rewards and the punishment, I need to make my boss happy. Making my boss happy and delivering my piece is more important than the total mission—that's my boss's job anyway.
- **I need to defend my turf.** There's no incentive for me to share responsibility or information with others who report to my boss. I won't get credit, and if delegating makes the overall result better, I'll just look expendable. So I need to defend my turf.
- **I'll base my teamwork on reciprocity.** Since I'm most interested in delivering my piece to my boss, I'll help you only if you can help me. If my helping you will make my contribution look weaker, then I'll pass.

➤ **It's my boss's job to keep me happy.** If I'm not happy with my job or with the environment, it's my boss's job to fix that. I'm just a worker bee.

➤ **Instead of working with the team to make decisions, I'll just sell my ideas to my boss.** My boss makes all the decisions. So when we need to make a group decision, I have to be there to defend my interests. My boss's decisions are part of a zero-sum game, and I have to get my share.

➤ **I must cover my ass.** In cases where I could get criticized by my boss, I need to cover myself so I can blame others on the team should something go wrong.

Do you want this person working for you? I don't, and neither do heroic managers. They want employees who will take initiative and solve problems; it's just that they don't realize they are destroying initiative by taking ownership of the team's output.

Even worse, heroic leadership creates a feedback loop in which heroic managers create the exact opposite of what they want. In their book *Power Up*, authors David Bradford and Allan Cohen identify a vicious circle caused by heroic leadership (see Figure 2.1).

This diagram shows what happens to a team under the management of a heroic leader. The leader takes over responsibility for the team deliverables and uses a system of cookies (rewards) and slaps (punishments) to get employees to deliver their portion of the job. Recognizing the game, the employees focus on their portion of the job and compete for cookies while covering themselves to avoid slaps. The leader complains that no one on the team is willing to take a leadership role and takes away even more responsibility from the team.

These leaders complain about their tremendous workload and about the fact that no one on the team will show initiative. They blame today's workforce, the culture of entitlement, or the employees. This cycle shows that their heroic leadership style is the problem.

To create the kind of collaboration that can overcome a layoff, you'll need to move beyond heroic leadership. You'll need to create

FIGURE
2.1

THE HEROIC MANAGEMENT TRAP

The heroic leader collects input and makes
decisions, while issuing cookies and slaps

In the absence
of team initiative,
the heroic leader
takes on even more
responsibility

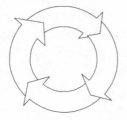

The team members
reduce their focus to
their individual jobs
and adopt a cover-my-
ass mentality

The heroic leader complains that nobody
will take ownership or show initiative

a team that recognizes your role as the manager but also shares
responsibility for results.

WHEN TO BE A HERO

There are times when it is necessary to take full responsibility
for the team's results and hand out assignments. These are usually emergency situations. Think of heroic leadership the way you
think of open-heart surgery—you do it only when there is no other
choice. There is always a cost associated with taking a heroic leadership stance. People will become dependent on you, and teamwork
will break down. However, sometimes you need to pay that price
to move the team past a difficult time. The following situations are
examples of when heroic leadership may be necessary.

A Desperate Turnaround

You don't have time to implement a shared-responsibility environment if you are in a floundering company with high expenses and
one month of cash in the bank. You need to fix the situation now. In

cases like this, you need to take responsibility away from the team and dictate the recovery plan. You can always restore responsibility at a later date, when the company has stabilized.

Steve Jobs walked into a situation like this when he took over Apple in 1997. A vice president of a company that was thinking of buying Apple said that whoever took over Apple would need to "go over there with a calculator and a hatchet." Jobs filled this role. At Apple, Jobs found a company that could not control its spending or manufacture its products. It was a company that still had dreams of conquering the world, yet it couldn't manufacture a computer.

Jobs changed all that. He sacrificed Apple's largest sacred cow—the Apple Newton, a PDA that the market had rejected. He also killed most of the product line and focused the company on two product lines aimed at the home market and graphic designers. And he did all of this in the classic heroic management style.

Jobs was also a fanatical micromanager. He approved minute details like the arrangement of buttons on the Mac OS interface. He ruled the company fiercely, and several executives left because they could not stand working for him. However, he got the job done.

Many managers use stories like this to justify a heroic style, but they forget the context for Jobs's success. He had walked into an emergency situation—a turnaround. The company's survival was at stake.

Do not confuse a turnaround with a layoff situation. In a layoff recovery, group survival is rarely at stake. If the group were going to be disbanded, it would have been cut during the layoff. Most groups that survive a layoff are not cash starved. The group will get paid and survive. The group doesn't need a hero; it needs a leader. Being a heroic leader is a tool of last resort. Managers who walk in and dictate actions damage the team. Sometimes this damage is necessary for survival, but this is rare.

An Emergency Deadline

You may run a group that needs to deliver services immediately or that deals with a critical deadline. Newspapers must hit a daily deadline. Service organizations often have contractual response times.

In cases like this you may need to make snap decisions and take a heroic role. However, you should establish parameters with your group that limit the kinds of decisions team members can push up to you. Be clear about the types of decisions you'll make and the ones the team will make. Then stick to that policy.

An Untrained Team

In some situations your team may not have the training or experience to help with the decision making. In such cases you should take over the decision making as you train your team members. When you do this, lay out a training path and tell them that you expect them to participate in these decisions in the future. That way you can ease yourself out of the heroic role.

Given that most of the leadership examples available are heroic, where can we find examples of the leadership that will demonstrate how to create a collaborative team? We need to look outside of business for a better model and examine volunteer community organizations instead.

CREATING SHARED LEADERSHIP

Volunteer organizations such as the PTA, children's sports leagues, and local political campaigns are excellent models of shared leadership. A leader of a volunteer organization needs to create an attractive environment where people feel they can make a difference and their efforts are appreciated.

Leaders of volunteers cannot threaten to fire people, reprimand them, or pass them over for a promotion. In fact, if they try to use the tactics often employed in business, they soon find that their organization shrinks and disappears. Why? Because people are drawn to volunteer organizations or public causes out of a sense of shared vision or common beliefs and interests. Unlike the world of employment, they are not obligated to give their time and talent out of the need for a paycheck and benefits. They are looking for collaboration, not another boss.

This is a key point. People don't want another boss outside of work—frankly, they often don't want a boss at work either. The entire power relationship between most bosses and employees is degrading and uninspiring. People become invested when they work in a collaborative environment. There are several essential steps that create this kind of environment.

Push Responsibility Down into the Team

Your first job as a manager is to make sure that everyone on the team feels responsibility for the team's performance. People will disengage if they feel they are simply part of your plan. Make sure you delegate responsibility and ownership to the team.

Consider the case of an employee who is appointed as group leader. This is a classic case in which someone has responsibility for making the group run smoothly but has no official position of power. A group leader who says "I want to improve our performance, and I need you to do this or that" will get nowhere. The other team members will be resentful and will resist being directed. A leader who says "Let's improve how we perform by doing this" will attract more than enough help.

In the first case, the leader is taking charge of the team's performance and is telling others what to do to ensure that performance. In the second case, the leader has invited other people to be part of what the group is about to create. They all feel responsible for making it happen, and they work together to create an organization. When that organization is in place, all the people on the team will feel a sense of accomplishment.

The group leader plays a critical role. The team will not improve if the leader doesn't suggest that improvement is possible and provide the energy to get it going. But the team will also not make any changes if the leader refuses to share the act of creation. The leader must make it clear that the entire team is responsible for delivering results together.

Some managers argue against this idea. They say that because their boss expects them to deliver results, they do in fact have final responsibility for the team's results. They argue that to pretend the team is responsible would be an obvious ruse.

Such managers miss an important point. Their boss expects them to deliver results—not a leadership approach. As long as managers can deliver the results they promise, their boss will usually be happy (barring micromanagement from above). Leaders are responsible for creating a team that delivers the results. The best way to do that is to share responsibility with the team members. Remember that there is a huge difference between saying "You go do it" and "Let's go do it." Leaders who say "Let's go do it" create a high degree of collaboration.

Make Team Decisions as a Team

Decisions that affect the way the team works are decisions that should be made by the team. This takes more time in the short run because creating consensus is a time-consuming process. It saves huge amounts of time in the long run, however, because the decisions are likely to be better and the team buys into the decisions.

Your leadership is essential during the decision-making process. Naturally, you will be an influential member of the group, so you need to use your power lightly. You should help the group create a list of options and help them analyze the options to unearth the best solution.

You need to be an active participant in the discussion, and you must be willing to support the team's final decision. If the team insists on coming to a decision that you cannot support, veto the decision and work with the team to create another one. However, be very careful with vetoes! You can destroy the collaboration process by overriding group decisions. People will realize that you are not walking the walk of collaboration, and they will stop participating. No one wants to play a game they feel is rigged.

Before you issue a veto, make sure you do the following:

+ **Remember that teams are usually right.** I've hired many people in my career, and most of my hires were great because I respected the input of team members. In the cases in which I made bad hires, it was always because I had either ignored advice from the team or not included the team in the process. Your team is likely to be correct in its analysis—you should give it the benefit of the doubt.
+ **Make your position clear in the discussions.** Your team needs to know where you stand during the debate. If you absolutely cannot support a decision, the team needs to know this is not a viable approach to the problem.

Do not let the team members come to a decision without your input and then override them. This will destroy any hope of creating a collaborative environment. If the team is leaning in a direction you cannot support, be direct. You can say something like, "Look, I can't do that. My experience tells me this is a failure path, and I would feel foolish trying to follow it. Can we come up with something else?" A team that ignores such an obvious statement should not be surprised when you overrule the team decision.

Also, if you override a group decision, openly acknowledge that fact. Be honest with your team. If you cannot support its decision, acknowledge the fact that you are overriding the team and that you don't intend to make it a habit. At your meetings, explain again why you are not comfortable supporting the decision and then put the issue back on the table to come to an acceptable solution. You can have this kind of discussion successfully if you have built up enough trust with your team.

Your team's ability to make collaborative decisions is critical to the rest of the rebuilding process. The team will be developing a mission statement, creating plans, and defining roles. You will get high-quality decisions with strong buy-in when the team makes the decisions.

EMBRACE DISSENSION

love parties, and I think I have a good memory. I can remember almost anything someone said in a conversation, almost verbatim. I cannot tell you what the person was wearing. That's my wife's job. She and I can attend the same event, and because we filter the world differently we remember different details.

We all have these filters, because the world has too much information for us to process it all. Our personal filters were formed when we were two to four years old, and we can't look at the world without them. These filters are the reason you need to embrace dissension in your team meetings.

Each person in a meeting brings a different perspective and a different set of filters to the meeting. Each person has different priorities and thinks about different things. Each person has a valuable piece of the puzzle and would be happy to share it with you as long as you don't shut him or her down.

Despite the value of multiple perspectives, many of us get impatient with too many perspectives. We want to get to the point and decide on that all-important next step. We think we can clearly see the world and, based on our view of the world, we know what to do.

Except that we don't clearly see the world. We see the world through the small pinhole that is our filter. Others see the world through their own small pinhole. We get a complete picture of the problem when we combine all these perspectives.

The key to gracefully handling dissension is not to let our egos get wrapped up in the decision. We all like to think we're pretty smart and we can pull the right answer out of the air. The danger is that we often connect the acceptance of our idea with the acceptance of us. This is a dangerous situation, because if we interpret the rejection of our idea as a personal rejection, we are going to work hard to defend it. After all, we're defending our self-worth at that point.

When we disconnect our ego from the idea, we will be open to hearing about the holes that others see in it. We are able to embrace dissension as a process that improves our idea, rather than a process that damages our self-worth. When our people see our openness to dissension, they will be willing to help improve the ideas on the table, and when they see us modeling an openness to new ideas, they will be open themselves.

Embrace dissension. The only thing you have to lose is a bad idea.

Replace Rewards and Punishments with Recognition and Natural Consequences

If you punish or reward another person, then your relationship to that person is based on power and fear. Pure and simple. This kind of relationship is acceptable in certain cases, such as with parents and young children, sergeants and soldiers, or prison guards and prisoners. It can even work in the case of a supervisor and unskilled laborers.

This approach will not work in the relationship between a manager and a highly educated knowledge worker. You cannot force someone to think. Companies that try to bully people into thinking or doing creative work lose to companies where people give their time as part of an equal relationship. Companies that draw the best out of people win in the marketplace.

Great managers know that recognition is a powerful motivator. People love to be recognized for their work. It is not even necessary that the recognition come from a source of authority. Recognition from one's peers is just as exciting. Volunteer organizations spend tremendous amounts of energy recognizing people and thanking them for their contributions. This is because recognition is one of the few things a volunteer organization can offer its supporters. It's important not to confuse recognition with bonuses or other incentives managers offer employees. Recognition is a sincere way of saying "Thank you." Sometimes saying "Thank you" is all you need.

While great managers don't use punishment to motivate employees, they do discuss the natural consequences of a situation. People are often strongly motivated to avoid negative consequences. For example, many journalism students work hard to publish a daily college newspaper. They take classes during the day and then work late into the night making sure the daily newspaper is ready for the next morning. There are no punishments in place if the newspaper doesn't get published—since their contribution is voluntary, they will not be fired or lose income. However, there are tremendous natural negative consequences. If a college newspaper missed the deadline, it would irrevocably harm the newspaper's reputation and anger its readers. It would hurt the team's pride and reputation. This is an example in which natural consequences, rather than punishment, motivate people.

It's important that you make the whole picture clear to your team so each member takes personal responsibility for both the positive and negative consequences of his or her actions.

You need to create a relationship with your team based on mutual equality that recognizes your roles. As a manager, it's your job to provide focus, help, and leadership to the team. Your employees' role is to provide expertise to help the team achieve its goals. Together, you need to come to an agreement in which the company and the employees feel it's in their best interests to continue the relationship.

Make Employees Responsible for Themselves

Some managers develop a messianic approach to their employees. They see themselves as "The One" who will keep people happy and safe in a turbulent corporate environment. They embrace their inner heroic manager and take personal responsibility for their employees' happiness and careers. This is the path to failure; these managers really don't understand their role in a tough situation.

As a manager, you are your employees' mentor, coach, and helper. If the team is unhappy about something—say, a lack of bonuses— then it's your job to help the team solve the problem. It is not your job to take on the problem as your own and carry it up the management chain.

The key is not making the team's problem your personal responsibility. Make it a team problem and use your access to upper management as a resource. Part of the plan may include your communicating with your management, but this needs to be done within the context of a plan your team created with you.

For example, I once led a team of engineers in a company that allowed all its engineers to go to one conference a year. The problem was, this team only had one conference that applied to its expertise, and upper management claimed it could not send the whole team.

I went to our director and found out that he believed it would be too expensive to send the team, so I made a deal: "If I can do the whole trip for under $10,000 can we go?" The director said, "Yes."

I told my team about the plan, and we worked together to put together a $10,000 trip. We traveled over Saturday, shared cars, and doubled up in cheap hotel rooms. ("What's that stain on the wall?") We pulled together as a team and had a great time on the trip.

I could have made it my job to get the team to the conference or to listen to them complain and feel their pain (and perhaps give up the conference myself in solidarity). Instead, I got the information we needed from upper management and then worked with the team to implement a plan.

You give employees power when you make them responsible for their own job satisfaction. They then feel they can influence the organization and direct their careers—something they can't do when you hold all the power in your hands and they are dependent on you.

Make Independent Decisions

Managers serve as a communication conduit between upper management and their teams. However, some managers make the mistake of becoming mouthpieces for upper management. When they do this, they lose their independence and risk losing the team's respect.

One high-tech manager learned this the hard way when he tried to sell upper management's spin to his team. The Fourth of July fell on a Thursday, and the company had Friday off as a holiday. Upper management announced that everyone would be required to take the preceding Monday through Wednesday off as vacation. They did this to remove the debt of accrued vacation from the books so the company could invest in a new customer-support organization without hurting profitability. Upper management told the managers to spin the forced vacation as a needed rest for all of their recent hard work.

The new manager blindly told this ridiculous story to his team. He looked like an idiot and lost their respect by repeating such a stupid story. His team turned on him and was very upset with the policy. A more experienced manager in the group ignored the story and explained to her team that the policy, though unpopular, created money for a new customer-support organization—and her people accepted the news gracefully.

It's important to remember that upper management is usually disconnected from the front lines. This causes these managers to say and do things that are irrelevant or even damaging. Make sure your team gets the information it needs, and don't get in the middle. Remember that it's your job to gather organizational information for the team. Information is different from raw data. You need to filter and organize data so that it becomes useful information. You need to use your judgment to make sure the information your team receives helps it do its job.

It is not your job to protect the team members from important information that would upset them. If your manager tells you that the team's workload will increase by 150 percent next quarter, and there are no more resources, you need to bring this to the team so that it can figure out how to respond to the challenge. This news will likely upset people, but as independent adults they need to know what's happening.

ALWAYS, ALWAYS, ALWAYS, ALWAYS TELL THE TRUTH

Your team members want to know three things about you: Who are you? Where are you going? Can they trust you? All the work we discuss in this book, and all the work that will happen once the layoff is a memory, can happen only after your team members have gotten their answers, and none of this work can happen if they don't trust you.

You can earn their trust only by telling the truth. So always tell the truth.

I'm not suggesting that you share inappropriate information. We managers know many things that should not get around. We know about the embarrassing medical condition that allows one of our team members to avoid having a hotel roommate at conferences. We know everyone's salary. We know why that guy was really fired. We know layoffs are coming, we know the day, and we know whom we're going to cut. We can't share this information.

On the other hand, there is no need to lie. If there are layoffs in the works, it makes no sense for us to say that there aren't. If we don't know whether a cost-cutting measure is permanent, we shouldn't give the impression that it's temporary. Most important, when we don't know the answer to a question, we should truthfully say that we don't know.

We all respond to authentic people, because none of us wants to spend time parsing words and body language to figure out what the boss really means. If you habitually tell the truth, your team will know. Once they know you tell the truth, they'll trust you. Once you have their trust, you can accomplish anything.

On the other hand, if your boss always makes predictions like this and is always wrong, you should wait before bringing this unfiltered data to the team.

Winning with Collaborative Leadership

Shifting your style from heroic leadership to collaborative leadership is hard work. You need to think differently, give up control, and trust your team to perform. People don't like change. If you have been a heroic manager, your team will try to get you to revert to Captain Kirk. Your employees may be uncomfortable with their new responsibility, and your boss may not understand why you are giving away power. You need to be clear about the benefits of a new management style to embrace it fully and educate others. You need to know what positive things you can expect from all this work so that you are motivated to make the change.

The most valuable thing about collaborative leadership is the employee attitude you can create. Here is what you hear from the members of a collaborative team:

+ "I'm responsible for the team's results. It's my job to do whatever I can to help the team meet deadlines and complete projects."
+ "Achieving our results is the most important thing. If the team achieves its results, I will get the recognition that I want, and I'll feel that I've done a good job. So if I need to sacrifice a bit to make it happen, I know that I'll win in the long run."
+ "I need to share my talents and do what is best for the team. I will seek out ways to help others on the team achieve their goals. If there is a situation where someone else is better suited to do a job, then I will seek out that person's feedback and involvement."
+ "I'm an independent person—I'm responsible for myself and my career."

- "My manager is my coach and partner—I use my manager as a mentor and take advantage of the resources he or she can provide; however, I make my own decisions and guide my own career."
- "I trust my manager and my teammates—I believe in telling it like it is and facing problems head on. When there is a mistake, I work with my manager and my team to fix the problem and move on."

Would you like to have this type of employee on your team? Of course you would. You can create an environment that creates and attracts these kinds of people. And the best thing about creating an environment like this is that you will get personal benefits as well. Here are the wages for creating a collaborative team:

- **Lower personal stress.** You'll experience less stress if you don't feel responsible for everything and everyone in your department. In the end, it is thankless work. Being a parent for five to fifteen adults is a terrible job.
- **A high-performing unit.** Employees who are internally motivated and who work out of a sense of personal satisfaction will perform better than those who are being monitored and controlled.
- **Time for high-value activities.** You can focus on higher-level management activities such as coaching, collaborating with your boss, and strategic planning when you can trust your team to do the daily work.
- **More rewarding work.** Imagine that your job is to help people reach their highest potential. This is much more rewarding than chasing people, checking off tasks, and settling petty disputes.

Creating a collaborative environment is a lot of work. It can be scary to let go of control, and you'll need to develop a new mindset and skills. However, the difference between guiding people and pushing people is worth the effort.

CHALLENGES TO COLLABORATIVE LEADERSHIP

There was once a senior manager with a boss who was authoritative. In watching the senior manager interact with his team, the boss commented to him that "your people love you like a father." The senior manager was pleased until he realized that his boss did not intend this as a compliment.

You will have many challenges like these as you implement a collaborative work environment. Most people are accustomed to a heroic manager who will tell them what to do. They feel uncomfortable with managers who push responsibility down to them, and they will push back. In addition, upper-level managers, who are often heroic, will sometimes see a collaborative style as weak. These challenges from your organization come in several different categories.

Teams May Not Be Ready for Shared Leadership

This problem usually strikes low-trust environments where the culture of the company, the previous manager, or the layoffs themselves have conveyed to people that their input is unwelcome. In these situations, pushing responsibility onto the team creates blank looks and uncomfortable glances.

Sometimes a team is ready to engage in the issues, but the team members are not ready to put the good of the team ahead of their own agendas. In this case you'll find that arguments tend to turn personal and that people attach their egos to their ideas.

The most complicated issues have to do with roles and responsibilities. It is very difficult for people to separate their own well-being from the team decision about roles. Someone who is adept at a specific skill might argue that his or her skill is the most important on the team. You will need to test the team members' commitment to the team mission before you ask them to take on difficult issues such as their individual roles.

If your team cannot handle shared responsibility yet, take a gradual approach. Give the team a simple group decision to discuss and see how they do. If they manage that decision, you can present them with more complicated issues. Keep pushing as much responsibility as you can down onto the team to stretch its ability to handle extremely complex issues.

Employees May Not Want the Responsibility

I once had an employee who resisted responsibility. We were installing new computer equipment, and it was his job to purchase the equipment and manage the installation. Though I had to sign off on the purchase, I wanted him to make the decision about what equipment to buy. He had the expertise to make the decision, but he wouldn't do it. Instead, he would lay the options out in front of me and ask me to pick.

As a manager, I tried to help him through the decision, so I would point to an option and ask, "Well, what if we went with this one?" At that point, he would shake his head, look away, and say, "Well, we could go with that one. You're the boss." It was maddening because it was obvious that he had preferences—he just wouldn't share them.

He had come from a large computer company that had gone through many layoffs and had become extremely bureaucratic. Everyone there had been in CMA ("Cover My Ass") mode. Because of this background, this employee did not want to stick his neck out to make a decision. He did not want to take responsibility for decisions because he had been trained not to.

As a manager, you may have to retrain these types of team members. Do not make their decisions for them. Keep pushing the decision back to them and ask them to make a choice. After I repeatedly refused to make the decision, my employee was eventually forced to do his own analysis and make his own decision. It was a much better decision than I could have made.

You may see this kind of behavior when you are moving toward sharing responsibility with your team. The team will argue a point and then ask you to make the decision. Or when you ask for ideas, you may get silence. These are cases in which employees are accustomed to having a parent instead of a manager. They silently hope you'll take back the reins and tell them what to do.

When you see these behaviors, you need to make it clear that you want the team to make decisions together because you are smarter collectively than any single person on the team—even a high-level performer. Stick to your guns and refuse to take back the responsibility you've given to your team. Eventually, some of your team members will respond and bring the others along.

You May Not Be Walking the Talk

Managers often say that they want to create a shared-responsibility environment, but they then take back the reins when decisions don't go their way or when the going gets tough.

Managers who do this often try to give the impression that they are letting the team make the decision when in reality they've already made the decision and want the team to endorse it. Some managers will try to do this by using the Socratic method. They will ask the team questions that appear to be open-ended but that actually have a specific correct answer.

You can see this difference between teachers who are good at leading class discussions and those who are not. The good ones will ask an open-ended question like "How would you have handled this situation?" They'll use follow-up questions to get the students to clarify their responses, and they may try to get the students to debate the possible points.

However, other teachers ask questions with a specific answer in mind. For example, they'll ask, "What's the most important reason for starting a business?"

One student will say, "A large number of customers?"

"Well . . . that's important too. . . ," the teacher says—obviously the wrong answer.

"Cheap labor?"

"Also important . . ."—but again, not the right answer.

"Your passion for the product?"

"Exactly! You've got to have passion to succeed!"

Ding-ding-ding-ding-ding! Thank you for playing!

Students will quickly turn off when presented with this kind of "class participation." Managers will take this kind of approach to give the impression that they are letting the group make the decision. But everyone knows it's a sham.

When you push responsibility for decisions down onto your team, you need to walk the talk. While you need to be an active participant in the discussion, you have to be careful not to overshadow the conversation. People will be watching your every move. If you frown, raise your voice, or pick on anyone's answer, your team will shut down and acquiesce to your opinion.

Your Team Might Not Believe You're Serious

This is similar to the problem just discussed, but in this case you are doing your best to keep the decision in the hands of the team. However, if your company has a directive culture, or if other managers have been directive, your team may not believe that you really want them to make decisions. They'll respond to your approach the same way they would if there was a hundred-dollar bill in front of them with a string attached to it. They'll halfheartedly go along with it, expecting the bill to be yanked away at the last moment. There is no short-term solution to this problem. You can only make it clear that you are serious and keep demonstrating your good faith. Eventually, they'll believe you.

Your Boss May Not Support What You Are Doing

This can be a serious problem in the case of a boss who wants to micromanage your leadership style. Many managers have never seen this style of management and may perceive it to be soft and unproductive. The best thing you can do in situations like these is to try to move your boss toward a results-oriented relationship. You can make a deal offering to deliver what your boss wants to see in exchange for some freedom in how to deliver it.

Collaborative leadership is counterintuitive. People naturally assume that leaders will create the ideas and tell others what to do. Our culture has created an environment where this is the expected behavior. When you work to implement a collaborative style, you will naturally get resistance from well-meaning people who genuinely have no idea what you are trying to accomplish.

By sticking to your guns and encouraging growth in your people and your teams, you will create highly trusting, productive teams. Once people get a taste of collaborative management, they will want more, while your team's increased productivity will impress your boss.

This kind of management style is especially important as you work to bring your team through emotional recovery. You cannot order people to feel better ("The firings will continue until morale improves!"). You can make people feel better only by showing them that you will do your best for them and leading them back to productivity through your own example and your own caring.

Fostering
Emotional
Recovery

DURING THE 2003 war with Iraq, the U.S. Marines did something that you wouldn't expect of them. They instituted support groups on the battlefield. This was part of a new program to help soldiers avoid the psychological trauma that had been seen in earlier wars. The Marines trained their soldiers to take time after the action was over and talk about their feelings. This process was critical to individual recovery and team morale.

This type of "soft management" is critical following a layoff. As we discussed in the Introduction, layoffs can be emotional events. Sorrow, betrayal, grief, relief, and guilt can reach intense levels. Many people unconsciously equate their company with their family; their boss becomes their parent, and their coworkers are their siblings. This equation creates powerful feelings of dependence. Emotional dependence plus a layoff is a toxic mixture that needs to be drained before healing can begin and the group can move forward.

You are not a trained psychologist, and it's unlikely that you will be able to hire a professional facilitator for your group—particularly if the layoff occurred because your company was strapped for cash. You can, however, still create an environment where healing occurs. You can create an environment where people feel comfortable talking about their feelings and bringing them to the surface. You can help your team heal itself.

Emotional recovery is a major step toward rebuilding your team. Going through the healing process together is an excellent way for teams to share an important experience and rebuild the bonds that were broken. You can start to rebuild trust when your team understands that you care about its members as people rather than as resources.

EMOTIONAL BANK ACCOUNT

The emotional bank account, which was first described in Stephen Covey's landmark book *The 7 Habits of Highly Effective People*, is one of the most important concepts in human interaction. The emotional bank account measures the amount of trust that exists between two people.

Think of the emotional bank account as you would a regular bank account. You can make two kinds of transactions with this account—deposits and withdrawals. If you make more deposits than withdrawals, the account balance will go up, and if you make more withdrawals than deposits, the balance will go down.

Very little happens when you make a small withdrawal from an account with a large balance. The account goes down a little, but the balance remains healthy. When you make the same withdrawal from an overdrawn account, warning bells go off, the bank sends you nasty letters, and your transaction will not be approved.

The emotional bank account works the same way. It's important to keep a high emotional bank balance with people so that if you need to make a withdrawal (or you accidentally make one), the relationship will remain strong. There are managers who have maintained great relationships with people whom they have laid off because the emotional bank account was so high before the layoff that it withstood an enormous withdrawal.

You make deposits into someone else's account when you do or say things that improve the person's self-esteem. When you give someone a compliment, answer him kindly, or include her in a decision or conversation, you are making deposits into your emotional bank account with that person.

You also make deposits through your actions. When you go out of your way for someone, do her a favor, or think of him with a short note or thoughtful gift, you are making deposits. All these actions say, "You are important to me. You matter."

There is one little-used action that makes tremendous deposits into emotional bank accounts—an apology. When you make a mistake that hurts someone else, acknowledge the mistake, and apologize, you will often deposit more back into the account than was withdrawn in the first place. For example, saying "I was wrong to embarrass you in front of the group—I'm sorry" conveys a lot about the kind of person you are and whether the other person can trust you.

You make withdrawals from an emotional bank account when you do or say something that reduces another person's self-esteem. Criticism, intimidation, and angry responses are all withdrawals. When you ignore someone or make the person feel excluded from a group, you are making significant withdrawals.

You will completely drain the account by lying. If you are seen as a backstabber or as someone who will warp the truth to achieve a result, you will permanently damage your account with another person. You can also do similar damage by being inauthentic. If you put on a happy face when you know things are going poorly in the team, you will lose credibility with your team and drain emotional bank accounts.

There are emotional bank accounts between people and organizations as well. The questions you considered when you were surveying the damage all addressed issues that damage the emotional bank account between your company and your team members. If the trust has been breached between your employees and the company, as will happen during a layoff, the company will need to work for quite a while to rebuild that account. However, as the manager, you can build the account you have with your staff members more quickly than the company can. You will serve as the link that will help the company rebuild its account.

Emotional Deposits

It's your job to understand the status of your bank account with each person in your group and build it from there. Here are some things you can do to build your bank account with your team:

- **Habitually compliment people.** Whenever you feel good about something someone has done, express it. Say "Good job!" or just reply to an e-mail that communicates a positive result with the word "Outstanding!" These little, heartfelt compliments build your relationship with your team.
- **Ask for advice.** When you ask one of your team members for advice, you demonstrate your admiration and faith. When someone knows you respect and value his or her opinion, it improves that person's self-esteem and makes another deposit into the emotional bank account.

CREATE A SPOT BONUS

Since you've just had a layoff, it's unlikely that your company has a spot bonus program. So create one yourself.

Spot bonuses are quick, impromptu bonuses that you give when one of your team members does something well. They are an excellent way to recognize people without resorting to an "employee of the month" mentality. Bonuses range from dinner for two to $1,000 in various companies. But they can be much less expensive. For example, a coffee shop gift card for $20 makes a nice spot bonus. If you get your manager's buy-in, you can expense the $20. And if you can't get your manager's buy-in (cheap so-and-so!), you can buy the card yourself. After all, it's only $20, $10, or $5.

If you do buy your own card for a spot bonus, make sure that the fact that you spent your own money slips out into the team. They'll appreciate the recognition even more knowing that you paid for it yourself.

Use spot bonuses by catching people doing something right and then giving them a bonus in that moment. They'll appreciate the recognition, and you'll be sure to see more of the excellent behavior.

◆ **Learn about your employees.** When you take an active interest in people, you tell them that they are important. This is the basis of emotional deposits. Later in the chapter we will talk about the one-on-one meeting and how you can use it to learn about the people on your team and rebuild trust after a layoff.

◆ **Fulfill commitments.** When you do what you say you will do, you make another deposit in the bank account that you can use later. Following through on your commitments tells other people that you value them because you spend time on their issues.

Emotional Withdrawals

An empty or overdrawn emotional bank account is debilitating. When you have an empty bank account with someone, you need to walk on eggshells. You know that every comment will be taken in the worst way possible and that the person will not trust your good intentions.

When you have a low bank account with someone, that individual will tend to take three steps when reviewing your actions:

1. **Note infractions.** If you arrive late to a meeting, the individual may count it as a strike against you.
2. **Create unflattering stories.** The individual will think, "You were late to this meeting because you don't care about my time."
3. **Retreat from the relationship.** The individual will say, "You don't care about my time, so the heck with you."

You'll catch yourself following these three steps when you have a poor relationship with one of your team members as well. If you are following the three steps above with someone, give some thought as to why you are feeling this way about this particular employee or coworker. Your attitude is your responsibility, so think about things you can do to improve the relationship before the other party retreats.

Withdrawals from the emotional bank account happen as a result of many things. Here are some to watch for:

LEARN TO LISTEN

Having someone come into your office and start sobbing is one of the most uncomfortable events we face as managers. Some of us are natural healers, and we exude empathy and warmth. Others hide behind our desk and nudge a tissue box at the weeping person. The question remains, what do we do?

The key to handling this situation is to listen. Stephen Covey calls this giving the person "psychological oxygen." He calls it oxygen because none of us focuses very well on larger issues if we're not getting oxygen. The same is true of listening. People just can't calm down unless they feel they've been heard. You can help them by doing one thing and avoiding two things:

+ **Do listen and show that you're listening.** Nod. Lean forward. Say,"Uh-huh." Do what it takes to let the person know you're listening. Don't interrupt. Don't ask questions. Just let the person's situation wash over you.
+ **Do not provide solutions.** This is the hardest part of listening for some people (me included). Some of us want to fix problems. We think that someone is pouring his heart out as a way of solving the problem. This is not what's going on. The person is

simply trying to get another person to understand him. The gift of being heard is difficult to find. If we try to solve the problem, we have to start judging the situation, and if we're judging the situation, we aren't listening.

+ **Do not start talking about yourself.** We all want to talk about ourselves, especially in an uncomfortable situation where someone is weeping in our office. We want the discomfort to end. So we convince ourselves that we are connecting with the person by relating a story about something similar that happened to us. We are not. The person doesn't want to hear about us. The person wants to be heard. When you start talking about a similar situation in your biography, you are grabbing the oxygen mask off the person's face and saying, "Hey, let me have a hit of that."

Handling an emotionally upset person doesn't require a degree in psychology. All it requires is that you listen to the person and give him or her that precious oxygen. You are a manager, not a psychologist; just listen. This is one of those happy cases where the one thing you can do is the one thing that helps the situation.

+ **Chastising people.** You need to provide corrective feedback or information to help people perform. But if you provide that information in a way that demeans the other person, you are making a big withdrawal. Say you had an engineer who created some code with a defect in it. You could say one of the following:

"The XYZ component has a defect in it" or "You screwed up the XYZ component." Which do you think is a withdrawal?

✦ **Complaining about other employees.** Do not gossip about incompetence. While some foolish people will look at shared complaints about other people as emotional deposits (they feel like they are "in the know"), wise employees will not. When you complain about one employee to another, you make withdrawals from accounts with your best people, because they suspect that you're doing the same thing to them behind their backs.

✦ **Comparing employees to each other.** Once there was a manager who had an outstanding employee named Phil. Unfortunately, this manager would constantly use Phil as the example of perfection when talking to other employees: "Well, Phil does it this way," or "Phil did it that way." This manager eventually managed to turn an entire group against her through these constant withdrawals.

A manager in another company would intentionally pit his employees against each other in meetings. If Mary made a great presentation, he would say, "See, Jake. That's how you make a presentation. Why don't you have Mary show you how it's done?"

This manager believed that making employees compete improved the group's performance. Instead, it turned meetings into torture chambers where each person tried to do enough to avoid getting chastised but not so much as to be held up as an example.

This guy had no emotional bank account, and nobody was sorry to see him go.

HEALING ACTION PLAN

Before you can help your team through the difficult job of recovering from a layoff, you will need an emotional bank account. Establishing one can't be done overnight. If you realize that you have little or no balance in your accounts, then you can fix it in only one way: make more deposits than withdrawals over a period of time. Here are some ways to create a healing environment.

Lead with Your Heart and Follow with Your Head

Talking about emotions in a charged situation like a layoff is uncomfortable. We constantly worry about offending someone or making the emotional situation worse. That can cause us to adopt a "facts only" approach to talking about the layoff. We figure that if we stick to facts, and lead with facts, we'll stay on emotionally safe ground. So we talk in terms of the reasons for the layoff, the prospects for the future, and how things will be reorganized. In short, we stay in our heads.

This approach doesn't work. Your employees emotionally disconnect from you when you lead with your head, because they will be thinking about their feelings while you are talking about facts. Rather than seeming to be in control, managers who stay in their heads seem out of touch.

To avoid this, acknowledge the feelings first. For example, you might be tempted to say, "Let's think about ways to restructure the workload to handle losing Jesse and Mike." This is leading with your head.

A better approach would be "I know you are upset and frustrated by the layoff. I feel the same way. It seemed that we were just getting traction, and now we need to start again. Over the next couple of days, let's think about ways to restructure the workload to handle losing Jesse and Mike."

Be Authentic

As the expression goes, "You may as well start with the truth, because you're going to end with it." Employees know who's shoveling bull and who is being straight with them. They also know there's information you can't share. They're OK with that; they just don't want to listen to lies. They want you to be as open as possible when a layoff has happened.

One of the toughest questions you'll get is, "Are there going to be more layoffs?" You could say something such as, "There are no more layoffs in the foreseeable future." But you're better off admitting, "I don't know. I think we're all done for now, because my management says we're at a good head count. I assume it depends on how the company performs."

It's OK to give a true answer that isn't comforting. We sometimes feel we need to sugarcoat the truth to protect morale (another symptom of heroic leadership). However, employees respond better to open, honest communication that treats them as adults.

Understand the Stages of Grief

Psychologist Elisabeth Kübler-Ross showed us that people follow a predictable pattern when they are grieving. These are commonly called the *five stages of grief*. If you know the stages of grief, and can predict them, you can react more positively when you see them. You won't be caught thinking, "These people are nuts."

Here are the five stages of grief:

- **Denial.** People deny that they feel any loss at all. They take a "Let's get on with it" attitude. This is why admitting your own feelings of loss and frustration is so important and why a group meeting can help. Denial is a tough stage to decipher because so many people have been through so many layoffs that they may really be saying, "Let's get on with it." I've found that both emotions often get mixed together—people will be ready to get on with it and will be denying their feelings about losing a friend in the layoff.
- **Anger.** Suddenly the loss is apparent. Your employees may become angry with you, the company, each other, or themselves. They may say that the company is going downhill and that things will never improve. They may be angry that they were vulnerable to being hurt in the first place.
- **Bargaining.** People may try to strike deals: "If I do this, can I guarantee that we won't have more layoffs? If we hit our numbers, can we hire our people back?" People have seen the loss but are trying to figure out how to reverse it.
- **Depression.** Once it's apparent that things will never go back to the way they were, people become depressed about what has been lost.

�──➤ **Acceptance.** People are ready to move on and work within the new situation. They've accepted the loss and the realization that there is nothing to do now but make tomorrow better.

Share this framework with the team when you have your initial meeting to discuss the layoffs. People who have been aware of what has been happening are more likely to move through the phases quickly.

COMMUNICATION STRATEGIES

Whenever there is a national disaster, the airwaves become saturated with news. The news channels repeat the same five minutes of information twenty-four hours a day. People watch continuously, alert for any change or new tidbit of information. This insatiable desire for information exists after a layoff as well. Be sure to share all the information you can with your team. Encourage your team to ask questions so you can find out the answers for them.

Be discreet when discussing employees who are gone. Your people may ask you why certain individuals were laid off. They are trying to gauge whether they are vulnerable themselves. Do not discuss the failings of those who have left. It serves no purpose, and in addition to being disrespectful, it presents serious legal issues. Focus on the reasons people stayed rather than why others left. For example, you can say, "I was forced to make difficult choices about who stayed and who was let go. In the end, I chose to keep the people whom I felt would do the best job. I based the decision on your talents, skills, and approach to your job. It wouldn't be fair for me to get into specifics about anyone who has left, so I won't do it."

Hold a Quaker Meeting

You should provide a way for your employees to discuss how the layoff has affected them. You will want to do this within two or three days of the layoff event, once people have had time to digest what has happened.

Some companies hire trained facilitators to run this kind of meeting, but that is rare. Usually there are no resources available to help people work through the emotions of the layoff. However, there is a simple meeting format you can use without being a trained facilitator. It is easy to run and will help people express their feelings about the layoff. It's called a "Quaker meeting."

The Quaker meeting is a way for people to express how they feel about the layoff in an emotionally safe environment. The meeting is easy to manage because it uses silence as a key element and doesn't require professional facilitation.

In a Quaker meeting, you give a preamble about the fact that there has been a layoff and that people may want to share their thoughts about it with the group. Everyone then sits silently. This silence causes people to consider what has happened, and usually someone will be moved to speak. People speak one at a time and don't directly respond to each other. They simply share their individual thoughts or feelings.

The point of the meeting is not to discuss the viewpoints, or reasons for the layoff, but to give each person the honor of attention. Because nobody is allowed to discuss or critique the views communicated during the meeting, team members have an open space to express themselves without criticism or censorship. This is a highly healing process.

You should go over the ground rules of the meeting before it starts so that people understand there is no discussion at this point, simply acceptance. Eventually the meeting reaches a point where everyone who is going to speak has spoken. You should thank everyone for participating and ask participants to reflect on what should happen next. Some groups will want to go away and think about what was said, while others may want to discuss the feeling immediately. Others may want a break of a few minutes or a day before discussing the ideas and feedback that came up in the meeting. Different teams have different personalities. Your best approach is to let the team decide how to proceed.

You need to make a personal decision about whether you want to start the sharing process. You must be authentic. Take off your manager hat and be yourself. If you share something with the team, do it because you feel the need to share it, not because you feel you must start the process.

Remember, emotions that are bottled up will never die. They just fester until they come out in ways that hurt team members, damage morale, and thwart productivity. A Quaker meeting format gives people the space to share and express emotions. Your team will be in much better shape once you've cleaned up the emotional issues surrounding a layoff. The process will also bring you and the other team members closer together.

Hold One-on-One Meetings with Your Team

It is likely that your team members will have feelings or concerns that they don't want to discuss in a group setting. Use one-on-one meetings to have private conversations with your team. If you want to move faster, you can take two or three people a day out for coffee to talk about the layoff.

Naturally you should keep these meetings confidential. Let each person share his or her concerns with you and air feelings. Avoid defensiveness. Provide information whenever you can.

There is no one best way to bring people through a difficult process like a layoff recovery. You'll need to try a combination and variety of the methods outlined in this chapter. Your goal is to let people mourn their loss and recover from the instability in their life. People will be ready to look forward only after they have worked through these issues.

Remember that you are not a psychologist. You are a business partner, mentor, and coach. If your company has an employee assistance program, advise your people to use it as often as necessary. If your company does not have an employee assistance program, lend a listening ear and give people the space to help themselves work through the issues of the layoff.

Managers who can take a team through this process are truly great leaders and deserve the excellent teamwork that will result from being proactive. This kind of work is difficult, but it is the only way to help a distressed group of people work through their loss and become productive again.

DINE TOGETHER

Dining is the magic elixir of relationships. Like Dr. Mephisto's magic tonic, it is good for what ails you. It opens doors, cements relationships, and provides an environment where collaboration can flourish.

There is something about breaking bread with another person that says, in a very primal way, we are in the same tribe. We should be working together. Stephen Covey says that we should treat our family dinner table as an altar, because that's where the family gets built. The same can be said of the corner coffee shop or diner.

When your team gets hit with a layoff, make the time to dine with each person on your team. If you can, pay for the meal. If you can't, split the tab. Either way, get out there together and sit across the table from each other sharing a bowl of nachos. You'll learn things about your team member that you never knew, and your team member can learn about you.

Don't leave this one to chance. If you've just had a layoff, get out your calendar and set up a lunch date with each of your direct reports. Use the lunches to implement the "Assess the Damage" part of the layoff program. Meet with everyone quickly. Then, once the crisis is past, keep the lunch schedule going.

4

COLLABORATING WITH REMOTE EMPLOYEES

IF LEADING A team through a layoff is like brain surgery, then leading a remote team through a layoff is like performing brain surgery with one hand tied behind your back. It is the most difficult trick in your management repertoire.

There was a time, not so long ago, when managing a remote employee was an exotic experience. It was a demonstration of your power and skills as a manager leading a "Worldwide Organization," and it conjured up images of you jet-setting around the world, speaking many languages, adapting to local custom, and having your martinis shaken and not stirred.

Those days are gone. Today, managing a worldwide team is common, and managing a remote team is more a reflection of your company's desire to leverage a global workforce than of your managerial power. Gone also are the jet-setting images of the worldwide manager. These have been replaced with conference calls that start at 6:00 A.M. or 9:00 P.M. and political battles that seem to spin out of control.

Remote management, challenging as it is, becomes more challenging during a layoff. The skills don't change, and what you have to do doesn't change, but you lose the luxury of looking an employee in the eye and instead have to interpret tone over the phone or gaps in a conversation that suggest that the other person is either angry or has muted you.

In this chapter, you will learn how to chart a course through the minefield that is managing remote employees through a layoff.

Don't Be a Seagull

The first rule to being an effective remote manager is to not be a seagull. In his book *Leadership and the One-Minute Manager*, author Ken Blanchard tells us that a "seagull" manager implements a three-step strategy:

1. Fly in.
2. Crap all over everything.
3. Fly away.

Seagull managers break almost every rule of effective remote management. They have no relationship with their people. They communicate in snippets. They have a manic need to come in and change something, largely to prove to themselves that they are indeed the manager. Finally, they have no follow-up. Once they fly away, you can ignore them until they swoop back, and, having forgotten everything they crapped on last time, they crap on it again or choose new targets.

Employees respond to seagull managers by feeding them scraps and hoping they'll go away. They view the managerial visit as a temporary setback in the effort to get real work done. They know the seagull will use the tiny window of this visit to judge them, so they spend a week planning for the visit and making sure everything is set up for a smooth ride. They plan a nice dinner for the seagull; they take the seagull to the ball game; they tell the seagull what the seagull wants to hear. They wave bye-bye as the rental car pulls out of the lot and then finally get back to work.

We don't want to be seagulls.

The Five Steps and Remote Management

Managing remote employees is no different from managing local employees, except that it's much harder because the communication channel is so narrow. As we've seen from the constant expansion of the Internet, people need bandwidth to communicate effectively. If you have an old telephone modem, you can read a book over the Internet. If you have modern fiber optics, you can watch an HD movie.

When we sit in the same room as our team, we have all the bandwidth we need. We can see the smiles; we can notice the eye rolls; we can see how John glanced at Mary just before answering our question about the numbers. We can have lunch together every day if we want.

People are designed to build relationships through high-bandwidth contact. But when we become remote managers, our high-speed fiber optic connection drops down to what we can fit over a phone line, and that's hardly any information at all. We need to do two things to respond to this challenge:

1. **Acknowledge it.** Don't pretend we can use the same communication style we use with people who sit next to us. Accept that we are managing in different circumstances.
2. **Adjust to it**. Remote management is not impossible. It happens every day, and we can get quite good at it. We simply need to consciously adjust.

Fortunately, the basic five steps of management apply to remote teams as well as local teams. We need to collaborate, challenge, choose, connect, and coach. We just need to do them a little bit differently with remote teams.

As always, collaboration has to come first. Creating an environment of shared ownership is much more important in a remote situation than it is with a local team. Having your local team abdicate responsibility and ask you to weigh in on every decision is bad, but at least they can find you. If your remote employees do the same thing, their productivity will drop dramatically. I remember one manager telling me about his BlackBerry, "If I don't answer this thing, commerce stops." That's not good.

You need your remote employees to make their own decisions. They need to understand what's been delegated to them and which decisions they can make on their own. They need clear direction, clear measurement, and clear guidance on how the job is to be done. Then they need to be let loose.

Collaboration is critical for remote teams, because you need folks to implement a plan when you're not around. Folks who don't understand a plan, or agree with it, will find "more important" things to do. You need to make sure everyone is on board with the direction your team is taking, or you need to work with your employees to find a direction that works for everyone.

It's your job to build collaboration with remote teams, and the foundation of collaboration is the emotional bank account.

The Remote Emotional Bank Account

Like all relationships, our relationships with remote employees are based on trust. Trust is based on the emotional bank account, that sum of emotional deposits and withdrawals that tells us whether we are in good shape with another person.

We manage our emotional bank account with people by making deposits and avoiding withdrawals. Deposits are things we do or say that make other people feel good about themselves. Withdrawals are either things we do or say that make other people feel bad about themselves or things we do or say that break the trust of the other person.

The basics of the emotional bank account are the same for local and remote employees. Yet there is a key difference between a remote account and a local account, and that has to do with the account's ability to maintain its value and the corrosive effect of withdrawals.

All emotional bank accounts have a sievelike quality in that they lose value over time. Someone who says "But, I gave you a compliment last February" clearly doesn't understand this aspect of emotional bank accounts. All accounts leak value and must be constantly refilled.

Remote emotional bank accounts leak value faster than any other kind of account. The kind word you shared last week is forgotten as remote employees lead their lives—lives that do not include you. You need to expect that, and you need to account for the fact that every time you reengage with a remote team member the relationship is going to be in slightly worse shape than it was the last time you talked or visited. You always need to do some damage control at the beginning of a new interaction.

This damage control may be very light. It may amount to no more work than brushing dust off an unused desktop. This is usually the case when you communicate with the employee on a daily or nearly daily basis. You can pick up where you left off with a simple "How did your daughter's recital go last night?"

If you speak weekly, you may need to do a little more rebuilding. You might need to take some time to share how your week went and ask after your team member's week. You'll want to give a compliment for anything good that you heard about your team member's efforts. You simply want to get back in sync.

The amount of work goes up as time goes on, and it is different for every remote team member. Some team members might lose very little of their relationship with you over time; others might need constant reassurance. The key is to assume that the relationship will be no better after the hiatus than before it.

There is another aspect of remote teams that makes them more difficult to maintain than local ones, and that is the corrosive effect of withdrawals. When you work with someone locally, you can screw up occasionally. You might make an offhand remark that the person takes badly or have a bad moment when you snap. Being local, you can recover quickly from these events. You can apologize

RECOGNIZE THE POINT OF VIEW

Imagine that I'm your team member and I'm sitting across the table from you when I ask you to try an experiment with me. I say, "Point your finger at me and move it in a clockwise circle." You go along with the game, sticking out your finger and moving it in a clockwise circle. Then I say, "No. I want a clockwise circle." What went wrong?

The problem is that a finger that appears to be moving clockwise from your point of view is moving counterclockwise to someone sitting across the table. We both have a point of view, but nobody has a complete handle on the truth.

When you're working with your team, remember that we often confuse point of view with the truth. This is especially hard to remember with obvious things, like a clockwise circle. These simple issues seem so obvious to us that we could interpret someone else's different viewpoint as an attempt to sabotage the process.

Just as fish don't see the water, we don't see our point of view. We all think we see the world as it is and other folks are simply misinterpreting the obvious. We also take our point of view personally. If somebody threatens our point of view, we feel they are threatening us.

There are three steps you can use to deal with point-of-view issues. If you use these three steps whenever things get heated, you have a much better chance of avoiding the point-of-view battles:

1. **Recognize that you are in a point-of-view battle.** When it seems you're making no progress because the other person (not you, of course) is being stubborn and unrealistic, you are in a point-of-view battle.
2. **Ask the question "Why do you say that?"** You want to see the world through the other person's eyes as best you can so you can see why the other person believes he or she is being reasonable.
3. **Shut up and listen.** Sorry to be so blunt, but you really do need to shut up and listen. You have just asked the person to share something personal, a point of view. If you immediately shake your head and explain why the person is wrong, you have botched this step. Instead, really listen and try to paraphrase the other person's point of view to show that you did listen.

These three steps will keep you out of the danger of a point-of-view battle. But be careful: if you follow them you might find yourself being influenced by others as you understand their points of view.

and then go back to being the type of person who makes constant deposits.

Your apology, and your immediate reversion back to a more positive attitude, has two effects. It repays a little bit of the recent withdrawal—but even better, it seals the hole where the withdrawal pulled out some value.

This becomes painfully apparent in a remote situation, because what was a simple withdrawal, perhaps an answer you snapped back or a point that you cut off, becomes a large leak in your relationship with your employee. The single event can reverberate in that employee's mind until you're dealing with someone who hates your guts for reasons you can't remember. To understand why this happens, we need to look at what happens in a breakdown.

ANATOMY OF A BREAKDOWN

A breakdown is any disruption in the relationship between two people or two groups of people. It usually happens when the people are in separate organizations or are geographically remote from each other. It can start with something innocent, but the source doesn't matter. The steps that follow are the same.

Imagine two people or groups of people with a communication wall between them. The wall can be organizational (perhaps they're in different business units) or physical—one person in New England and the other in California. It doesn't matter how the communication wall is created; it simply matters that constant, close communication is not possible.

The situation is now ripe for the following, unhappy chain of events:

1. **Some garbage flies over the wall.** The nature of the garbage doesn't matter. The garbage can be a bad tone over the phone, an ignored e-mail, or a misunderstanding about what time to meet. All that matters is that the garbage flew over the wall and hit somebody.
2. **Someone makes up a story about the garbage and takes it personally.** Nature abhors a vacuum, especially a communication vacuum. Since there is a wall preventing easy communication, the person who got hit with the garbage makes up a story to explain it. This story always involves why the tossed garbage was

a personal attack of some sort. The story never gives the garbage tosser the benefit of the doubt.

3. **The person hit by the garbage withdraws from the relationship.** This is the final stage. At this point the person, who is now personally wounded by the garbage tossing, says, "The heck with them," and now the emotional bank account has an enormous hole with hard-earned goodwill spilling everywhere.

I was personally part of this story from perspective of the person being hit by garbage. I was selling on the East Coast for a large technology company and had a manager on the West Coast. I shared an office with another person who worked for this manager. Since we used our own cars for work, we got a car allowance to pay for gas and maintenance.

Our manager wanted us to fill out reports on all our sales calls, and we had fallen a bit behind on this paperwork. The garbage that came over the wall was an e-mail that said, "You guys need to get your call reports in. You wouldn't want to lose your car allowance, would you?"

We read the e-mail at about the same time and exploded. The story we told came to us immediately and included statements like "He doesn't know how hard we work," "He has no sense of priorities," "He hates people on the East Coast," "He's an idiot," "We already are looking at a tough year, and he's going to cut our pay," etc., etc., etc.

By the time we were done whipping ourselves into a frenzy, we were polishing our résumés and had declared that there was no way we could work for such a tyrant. In fact, both of us quit within six months.

This was obviously not the effect our manager had intended. Looking back on it rationally, I can see that it wasn't even possible for our manager to change our compensation plan in the middle of the year over something so trivial. I'll bet that he would have been astounded to see how much power he had exerted in a simple, off-hand comment. That's because he hadn't considered the stories we would write as a result of his comment.

We all invent stories when garbage comes flying over the wall. It's natural. Managers in a relationship are not immune. For example, if an employee misses a meeting with us, we can quickly decide that this is a passive-aggressive expression of the lack of respect this woman has always shown us. After all we've done for her! Etc., etc., etc.

The ultimate breakdown happens when the stories start to reverberate. The first bit of garbage flies over the wall and, enraged by the story he had created, the guy over there throws some garbage back. The woman on this side of the wall, who legitimately didn't know she had thrown the first bit of garbage, gets hit "for no good reason" and makes up her story: "He's a sexist." And then we're off to the races.

Wars literally get started because of this dynamic. The question is how to avoid them and fix them.

Avoiding Breakdowns

Sun Tzu tells us that it is more effective to avoid a battle than to win it, and the same is true of breakdowns. Fixing a breakdown requires an enormous amount of effort. It is better to avoid the breakdown. If we can't avoid the breakdown, then we need ways of getting the breakdown under control.

Use Massive and Positive Communication

The key to both avoiding breakdowns and fixing them quickly is fast, direct communication. This is why the United States and China created a hotline between Hawaii and Beijing. One of its first uses was to call the Chinese military to let them know that two U.S. military cargo planes were flying into China's airspace to deliver humanitarian aid to victims of the Sichuan earthquake. A U.S. airplane flying into Chinese airspace is exactly the type of garbage that can lead to escalating stories and large-scale conflict.

This is a simple rule of remote management: promote, support, and engage in massive communication. You are trying to re-create the feeling of being in the same office as your remote employees.

Many forms of conflict wouldn't happen if clear and constant communication had been going on. I doubt the manager in my story would have walked into my cube and said, "Get me those call reports or I'm cutting your car allowance." A large amount of ribbing and nagging would have gone on first. My manager would never have felt the need to resort to a threat to my income if he had been able to nag me incrementally. This incremental nagging is possible only because of the extensive communication that happens when two people are in the same office. Here are some specific ways to improve communication:

- **Use your phone.** Before they became marvels of mobile computing, cell phones were devices with a microphone and an earpiece, and people would use them to talk. In fact, we still can. Using your phone to speak to someone, instead of e-mailing, is one way to increase the amount of information traveling between you and your employee.

  Make an excuse to call your team members. E-mail may be more efficient, but it may not be more effective. Calling people gives you a chance to maximize the communication bandwidth and listen to the tone in their voice. Make sure you're talking to your team members at least once a week, but try for more. Remember that the relationship will only deteriorate when you are not talking.

- **Use the Internet.** E-mail, instant messaging, shared desktops, and social networking sites are all ways to effectively increase communication bandwidth. Use these tools. For example, instant messenger tools tell you when someone has come online. Take that opportunity to say "Good morning." The key to success here is to treat your "Good morning" habit as a social interaction and not as an indication that the "all-knowing and all-seeing leader" has duly noted your entrance. The chorus from "Santa Claus Is Coming to Town" gets creepy when applied to remote management.

Beware of the e-mail echo chamber. E-mail is the most dangerous form of communication invented by man. It gives you a higher chance of self-immolation than sending smoke signals. E-mail combines the informality of talk with the permanence of the written word.

Memos and letters were safer forms of communication. They had to be crafted. You wrote them with a pen. You chose your words carefully, and you wrote them with an eye toward posterity. Most important, they had no reply-all button.

E-mail is too quick. We write it when we're distracted. We stand in line at the coffee shop where some lady and her three screaming kids cut in front of us and then proceed to take fifteen

---

THINK BEFORE HITTING "REPLY"

There is a button in your life that is so horrible, so heinous, and so powerful in its reach and destructive capability that its use should be controlled by a double key system like the ones they use for nuclear warheads.

It is the reply button. The reply button has damaged more careers than any other piece of information technology. The only thing worse than the reply button is its Armageddon-inducing relative, the reply-to-all button.

Never use the reply button in anger. If you do, you are sure to write something that will come across as snarky, whiny, or angry. And if you send a snarky, whiny, angry e-mail to any of your employees, you can be sure that, if you are lucky, this employee will read the e-mail over and over again, fuming about the injustices of the world and your special role in them.

If you're not lucky, your employee will forward the e-mail to friends with the note, "This is what I put up with," and if you're really unlucky, your employee will forward the e-mail to coworkers and plot your demise.

And don't think that you can write an e-mail when you're angry and not have that anger spill through in word choice and tone. We are all much better writers than we think, especially when angry, and your hidden message of anger will come through.

What do you do when you get an e-mail that sets you off? The best thing to do is nothing. Just let it sit for a while, while you accomplish some other task. But, if the e-mail requires immediate attention, pick up the phone. Phone calls are ethereal—the words disappear as soon as they are spoken. They may not be forgotten, but they can't be forwarded (unless you leave a voice mail; don't do that either).

You will never regret the e-mail you don't send.

---

minutes to place an order, because the kids won't stop fighting over whether they should get a cookie with M&Ms on it, and we read an e-mail that says that the report we need Tuesday afternoon won't be ready until Tuesday morning, and we panic, and then we snap and write "Dammit! I want it on my desk Monday morning," not realizing that we've just ruined three people's weekends.

Now there's an e-mail floating around, evidence of the miserable jackass that we've become since we were promoted. The e-mail will be forwarded to family members to explain why the weekend is ruined. It will be talked about over lunch, with employees parsing it out on their BlackBerrys like it is some sort of sacred text. Finally, it will be forwarded to mymanagerisajerk.com. This never happened with memos.

Then, on Monday morning, we'll go back to work, having forgotten about the lady and her kids, and we'll wonder why everybody is so quiet on the conference call.

Watch out for e-mail. Never write it in a hurry. Never write a negative e-mail. Save negative comments for the phone. Nobody's career has ever been shortened by an unsent e-mail, so make the unsent e-mail your friend.

Catch Yourself Being Human

It is tempting to think that the "get hit by garbage/make up a story" dynamic is something that those people on the other side of the wall do all the time but that we are immune from. Alas, we are not. We are just as susceptible to making up stories as the next person.

Consider, for example, the e-mail that said, in essence, "Get me those call reports or I'm cutting your car allowance." This was not the product of a well-considered plan of influence. It's more likely that my manager was frustrated. It's very likely that my not sending call reports was, in fact, garbage that I had inadvertently thrown over the wall. Perhaps the story went, "Those guys on the East Coast think they're so smart. They don't respect me or my position.

All I ask is that they send me a lousy call report, and they can't even do that." Thus the e-mail that set us off was born.

We managers are humans, and humans fall into this pattern all too easily. Like all humans, we see the take-it-personally flaw easily when someone else is revealing it. Yet, when we are displaying it, we think we are simply responding to what's been handed to us. We think, "No! In this case I should be taking it personally."

Another method for avoiding breakdowns is similar to one for avoiding forest fires. If you don't want forest fires, don't set them. Similarly, if you don't want to have breakdowns, then don't break down yourself. Don't let yourself get caught up in taking other people's garbage personally.

When you find yourself falling into a breakdown situation with one of your team members, you need to do one of the hardest things in the human experience. You need to put yourself in the other person's shoes and think about it from that person's perspective. You need to see that you might be the problem here and that you cannot solve the problem by butting heads one more time.

Get an Outside Perspective

I have a friend who helps me through breakdown situations. I visit him and tell him what's happened in the breakdown, and then he generally says "You're full of crap" and then explains how I caused the problem or how my behavior is prolonging it.

We all need a friend like this. Most people will agree with us when we tell them a story of political woe. They'll agree that we were wronged, that we have every right to be angry, and that the other person, employees included, is a jerk. This might make us feel better, but it will not help us solve the problem.

We really need someone who will tell us that we are full of crap, help us analyze the problem from the other person's point of view, and then walk us back from the precipice. We need to be reminded that we are human and that we're having a human moment.

Only after we let go of the personal hurt, and the ego bruise that goes along with it, can we look at the situation from our employee's point of view and make the crucial phone call that will move us into the path of recovery. Until we're ready to listen humbly to why the other person is angry at us, we're not ready to help him or her get past the situation and move on to better things.

Never Ascribe Motive

Making up stories to explain other people's behavior happens so quickly and insidiously that we usually don't know we're doing it. The key to catching yourself is to notice when you're saying, "She's doing that because . . ."

When you ascribe motives to another person's actions, you are skating on the edge of a breakdown. It is the first sign that you are making up a story, and making up a story never helps the situation.

It is impossible to know why other people act the way they do. Sometimes even they don't know; that's the reason we have psychologists. You are not a psychologist—you are a manager. There is little to no chance that you are going to figure out other people's motivation. If they give you a motivation for their actions, believe them. If they don't give you a motivation, don't try to guess it. Talk about, and respond to, actions alone.

Breakdowns are hard to fix. Let's make sure that we aren't causing them or prolonging them.

Build an Enormous Account

Garbage is going to fly; it's inevitable. People are going to be late; jokes are going to be taken the wrong way; you'll reply to an e-mail in haste. We're human. We do these things. The key is to have an enormous bank account.

Take every opportunity to grow the account. Remember birthdays. Send praise whenever something good happens. Forward praise from other people. Visit people and eat with them. Have fun with your remote team members when you get to visit them. Deposit, deposit, deposit, deposit.

If you build a huge account, you'll be able to afford a slip. The account will take it, you'll be able to communicate again, and you'll get yourself back on track. Be kind to the bank account, and the bank account will be kind to you.

FIXING BREAKDOWNS

There is only one way to fix a breakdown. It's not easy, and it can be painful—but like setting a bone, it's the only way to heal the wound. You need to open communications wide and listen.

Poor communication is like darkness; it lets things grow that wouldn't grow in strong light. The only way to fix a breakdown is to throw the lines of communication wide open. In the best of all worlds, you should fly out to visit the person who is the other half of the breakdown. Face-to-face communication provides the widest possible bandwidth. It lets you see the other person's reactions, and it lets the other person see that you are not the monster created in his or her mind. It is a powerful resetting experience.

If you can't visit your partner in breakdown, then you'll at least need to set aside some time for a long, long phone call. There is a lot of work to do, and it won't get done if you're trying to fit the conversation into fifteen-minute slots.

Once you're in the room (or on the phone) with the person in breakdown, you need to step into the hardest part of the process. Stephen Covey calls this the "fifth habit of highly effective people": seeking to understand before you seek to be understood.

Your job at this point is to listen completely and openly to the person as he tells you how horrible you are. This is very difficult. What he says will be unjust. It will be bizarre. He will have come up with a story so fantastic that it no longer bears any relation to the original incident. You might start the conversation with, "It seems to me that you're angry at me." The goal is to get the person to feel comfortable enough to unburden himself on you.

This is not the time to defend yourself. It is true that you didn't mean what you wrote in that e-mail. It's true that you had a good reason for being upset. It's true that you have a side to this story. All these things are true, but they don't matter in the moment. All that matters is that you let your counterpart in conflict feel heard.

Use your active listening skills, open up, paraphrase back what you've heard, and finally, apologize where necessary. In the end, you both will probably end up apologizing, so you might as well go first.

You might, after you've fully understood the other person, share what it's been like for you . . . not to defend yourself but to reciprocate. It's not easy to bare one's soul, and your counterpart might have done quite a bit of soul baring. It's important that you reciprocate and let the other person know how you feel.

If this meeting has gone well, you should both feel that a weight has been lifted from your shoulders. You should feel cleansed and feel that you can start trusting this person again. Now is the time to start rebuilding the relationship by making emotional deposits.

You might just be back to zero balance, but it beats being overdrawn.

INCLUDING REMOTE TEAM MEMBERS IN DECISIONS

Creating an environment of collaboration and delegation is both critical and difficult in a remote environment. It's critical because you need your remote team members to execute their jobs without supervision, and if they don't believe in the plan it's easy for them to go off on their own and do their own thing. They might not do it intentionally (remember, we are not ascribing motives), but they might get distracted by what they believe is more important.

Remote buy-in is difficult for the same reason all remote relationships are difficult. The communication bandwidth is too narrow to make it easy to work together. There is also the problem of balancing the influence of remote employees with local ones. The remote employees know their local counterparts are likely to have more influence over you, because the local folks get to make their arguments after the conference call is over.

Fortunately, we live in a time where professionals manage remote collaboration all the time. The open source software movement, which gave us software such as Firefox and Linux, has developed ways of coming to decisions without the participants ever being together. We can borrow some of these techniques to help our remote employees feel connected to the group decision-making process.

Collaboration Through Conference Calls

Conference calls should never be more than thirty minutes long and should never be used for important debates. While the folks in the room can remain engaged for much longer, the folks on the speakerphone will soon tune out. They will be missing too much nonverbal communication to be an effective part of the process.

You can, however, have longer conference calls in cases where one person is presenting slides on a shared screen and transferring information. The one-way information flow is much easier to deliver over a speakerphone than a debate.

Speakerphone meetings require more preparation and discipline than face-to-face meetings in conference rooms. Each speakerphone meeting needs to have a written agenda so that remote participants can follow along and keep connected to the conversation. After each meeting a scribe must distribute notes about what was discussed, what questions are left open, and which action items were assigned.

These disciplines assure the remote participants that the conference call is a good use of time. There is nothing worse than being plugged into a conference call and listening to other people have a debate when you have no idea what they are talking about. It's demoralizing, and it won't help your relationship with your remote team members.

If you have a travel budget, spread your presence around your team when you have remote meetings. Let as many team members as possible have the opportunity to sit in the room with you during the meeting and let the folks back at your office feel remote.

Another Benefit of Collaborative Management

If you have avoided the trap of heroic management and have developed a truly collaborative team, you'll have a much easier time with remote team members and decisions, because nobody on your team will feel that he or she is trying to sell you on the idea. Instead, everyone will be focused on trying to sell the team. Having you geographically close to one set of team members will not give them a special advantage.

Of course, not all teams will become fully collaborative, and if that is the case with your team you need to rotate your physical presence in meetings if possible so that everyone feels he or she has gotten enough time with you.

Your job is to move your team to the point where it can make decisions without you. That way you won't need to fly all over the world making sure that commerce hasn't stopped. This improvement to your lifestyle is the ultimate benefit of a successful collaboration step.

PART 2

CREATING AN EXCITING CHALLENGE

Your second step is to take what you learned in the last few chapters and build an exciting challenge with your team.

This task can feel like fixing an engine while the car is driving down the highway. Your team certainly will be working during the weeks of the rebuilding process. That said, this process will help you focus your team. You may find that there are tasks your team is doing that don't need to be done. Anything you can take off the team's plate will improve its productivity in tackling more important problems.

The three tasks listed in the following chart each have a clear and specific deliverable. You should get each one done by the Friday of the week indicated. As you can see, these are SMART goals: specific, measurable, achievable, relevant, and time-bounded.

CHALLENGE

DELIVERABLE	DESCRIPTION	DATE
Have your team presented a stakeholder analysis report.	Lead your team through a stakeholder analysis process (see Chapter 5). Teach your team about the four stakeholders and how to discover what each stakeholder wants from your team. Show the analysis to your stakeholders and get their agreement.	Week 4
Publish a mission statement.	Lead your team through the mission-creation process (see Chapter 6). Have a training meeting to start the process. Help the team discuss the mission and lead the team through the mission-crafting process.	Week 5
Publish goals.	Help your team translate the mission and stakeholder analysis into SMART goals (see Chapter 7).	Week 6
Publish roles for your team.	Create a work flow for your team and define the roles and job descriptions that will make your team run smoothly. Share your ideas with the team and get feedback; then deliver the final role descriptions to your team (see Chapter 7).	Week 7

Now that you've got a team that's ready to collaborate, you must aim the team at a goal. A team is a team only if it's working toward a common purpose; otherwise it's just a group of people who happen to have the same boss.

In this section you will help your team orient itself in the company to understand its customers, suppliers, peers, and management. Gathering this data will give the team the information it needs to create its mission statement. The mission statement is the team's agreement about what it does and how it does it. It is a guide to help team members make their own decisions in concert with the rest of the team.

Once the team has oriented itself in the company and has written down its mission statement, it's time for the team to develop its goals. You'll help the team create SMART goals that give it specific and measurable targets.

There are three stages to this task, and remote employees must be taken into consideration as well. This section covers:

➔ Performing a stakeholder analysis
➔ Developing a compelling mission statement
➔ Defining goals
➔ Influencing remote employees

This step will move your team from being a group of individuals who want to work together to being a team with a common purpose, even when those individuals are scattered across the world.

Performing a Stakeholder Analysis

STAKEHOLDERS ARE GROUPS or individuals in the company who rely on your team. These groups, or their needs, can change dramatically after a layoff. Sales teams can suddenly start selling entirely new product lines or selling in new territories. Engineering projects may be canceled or might change. Some groups may disappear, and parts of their work may be spread across several preexisting teams. It's your team's job to figure out what each group needs now and how those groups measure results.

There are four types of stakeholders as shown in Figure 5.1:

+ **Management.** Management includes your manager and those above him or her. It's essential that you keep your management chain happy. Management expects your team to deliver what it promised in terms of services, revenue, and cost. This is particularly critical in a postlayoff organization that may be struggling to keep the doors open or rebuild confidence with customers and investors. Management also wants to receive reports that you are working well with the following three stakeholders.

✦ **Suppliers.** These are teams that provide your organization's inputs. For example, a supplier may provide parts to your manufacturing team. Suppliers can also be support organizations like the IT group. You can tell if an organization is a supplier if you need to wait for it to complete its function so your team can complete its function. Suppliers want notice of changes in your needs and feedback about how they are doing. They also want recognition for a job well done.

✦ **Customers.** These are groups that rely on your outputs. These groups can be either internal or external to your company. For example, customer-service departments support external customers, but they may also support an internal sales/marketing team. Customers want you to deliver on what they believe you promised. To avoid problems, it's important to be clear about what you can deliver when setting expectations.

✦ **Peer groups.** These are other groups in your company that perform functions similar to yours. For example, you may be on a marketing team that supports a software product line. Your

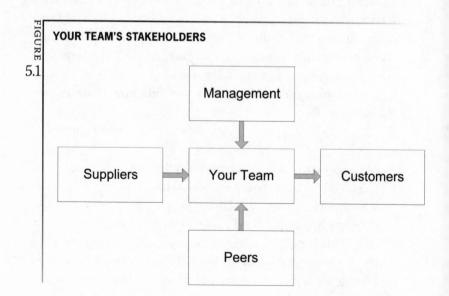

FIGURE 5.1

YOUR TEAM'S STAKEHOLDERS

Management

Suppliers → Your Team → Customers

Peers

DO AN 80/20 ANALYSIS

When you have fewer people on your team, you need to become more efficient. One way to do that is to conduct an 80/20 analysis on where your team is spending its time and where your team is getting its results.

In the general case the 80/20 rule says that 80 percent of your time will be taken up by 20 percent of your customers; conversely, 80 percent of your income will come from 20 percent of your customers. The 80/20 rule is a good rule of thumb to predict how resources such as time or money get divided among their sources or their users.

The beauty of an 80/20 analysis is that it shows you how to focus your team's attention. If you are a customer support team, you may find you are spending 80 percent of your time on 20 percent of your customers. Once you create a list of these customers, you can start asking questions about them. What do they have in common? What questions do they commonly ask? Do we have a way to be more effective at answering those questions?

The 80/20 analysis is one of the most powerful tools in business. It not only makes your team more effective, but if you mention it in a presentation to upper management they will be very impressed.

---

peers in marketing may be doing the same job but be supporting different product lines or territories. The managers of these groups may be peers of yours with the same boss, or they may simply have the same role in a different organization. Your peers want to remain informed and involved in any plans you implement after the layoff.

Your team must balance these various stakeholder relationships and keep a wide variety of people happy. A layoff can disrupt all of these relationships as the organization changes and regains its balance. A stakeholder analysis is the key to the recovery.

STAKEHOLDER ANALYSIS

The stakeholder analysis is a simple report that identifies the stakeholders and clarifies their needs. It captures and summarizes what your team members have learned. The report has one page for each stakeholder, and these pages are divided into three sections: primary contact(s), desired results, and measurement.

Primary Contact or Contacts

This is the person or persons in other groups or departments who interact with your team. In the case of management, the primary contact is usually one person. In the case of a complete support team, you will need to name all the people on that team. Obviously this part of the report can change dramatically in a layoff as people leave the company or are moved into other departments.

Desired Results

Desired results are what teams or individuals want to accomplish together. For example, let's say your group processes credit checks for the sales organization. The sales force is your customer. Your desired result may be "fast sales to creditworthy people." A quality assurance organization may have a manufacturer as a customer; thus the desired result might be "accurate quality tests delivered quickly."

You can also create a desired result with your suppliers. This allows you to give them a clear idea of what you expect.

Measurement

How will your stakeholder measure whether the desired result has been met? There are no goals without specific measurements. So in the case of "fast sales to creditworthy people," you may measure the turnaround time from your group to the sales force and the default rate on the deals. You can also use a quantifiable measurement to specify what you want from your suppliers. For example, your team may need five hundred widgets per month or customer phone calls returned within two hours. Establishing a measurement allows your team to set clear expectations for other teams and evaluate performance.

The answers to these questions may change as the company regroups after the layoff. Sometimes companies will throw out their organizational chart and start rebuilding from the top. In these cases it will take a while for the dust to settle and for people to know what they need. Of course, it's possible that none of these factors has changed. Many times companies simply reduce the size of all the groups but keep the relationships intact. The group relationships stay the same while the people change. Here is a sample form, created by a team of sales administrators to capture what the sales team wants them to do:

- Primary contact—Alice Smith, sales manager
- Desired results—Fast and profitable sales transactions
- Measurement—The sales administration (SA) team will check the creditworthiness of new clients within two working days of a request. The team will also create official price quotations and deliver them to potential customers within one day. In the last week of a quarter, the SA team will provide four-hour turnaround on quotes that can result in sales for that quarter.

The sales administration team now has a clear description of the relationship between its team and the salespeople. Alice Smith can tell her team to plan their work around the two-day, one-day, and four-hour delivery expectations from the sales team.

WORKING WITH YOUR TEAM

For a stakeholder analysis to be effective, you need to include your team in this process. Your team members work with people on other teams who can help them fill out the stakeholder report. You may find situations where different people on the same team ask for different results. It's better to get these cleared up now before misunderstandings cause problems.

The first step is to teach your team about stakeholders and the stakeholder analysis. Draw the stakeholders diagram on a white board and explain the different roles. Ask your folks to take note of which contacts and relationships have changed. Let them know that you are working to understand the new organization and that you need their help in doing so.

Your team needs to take ownership of its position in the company and of the job expected of it. Some teams imagine that you, the manager, should go out and investigate the landscape and tell them what to do. Don't do it! Push that responsibility down onto the team and stay in your role of agenda setter and facilitator.

Of course, you will also be part of this process. You need to fill out the stakeholder analysis form about your immediate boss, and you need to talk to your management counterparts in the stakeholder groups. Make your contribution a part of the overall process rather than the entire process.

Here are some questions you and your team can consider as you capture stakeholder information.

+ **Management.** Has your manager changed, or has the management above your manager changed? Does this change your charter or mission?
+ **Suppliers.** Can you get the information, materials, and services you need from the same places you got them before?
+ **Customers.** Do you have the same customers you had before? Do these customers still exist? Do they want more from you than before?
+ **Peer groups**. How were your peers affected? Will they want to share the workload with your group? Will your peers want to increase or decrease the workload on the teams?

Once you have an initial meeting with your team, follow up with your team members during the next week. Find out who has embraced the process and who is not interested in participating. Let people participate at their level of interest. Forcing team members to have information-gathering conversations is counterproductive. They are unlikely to gather anything useful.

Let your staff know that you will be using this information to make mission and goal decisions later and that the best way they

FOCUS ON THE FUTURE

When you start your stakeholder analysis with your team, you will identify customers and then go and visit them. This is a great start. Now there's just one question: What do you say when you meet with your customers? The best thing to do is to focus on the future.

When most people meet with their customers, they make the mistake of focusing on the present. They ask questions such as "How does your group work?" and "What are you doing today?" They sometimes touch upon the future with the question "What is your biggest challenge?" but that question falls short too. It's still about the biggest challenge today.

You can feel the energy get sucked out of the room with questions like these. The problems and challenges that come up every day are not interesting or exciting to them.

If you want to ask questions that excite your customer, ask, "What are your goals this year?" or "If you could wave a magic wand, what would next year look like?" The key is to talk about the future.

People love talking about the future. The future is full of possibility. The future is still shiny. The future is where they want to be. When you ask customers about the future, you tap into their dreams and aspirations. If you can help them get there, you become their best friend.

Once you've connected to your customer's vision for the future, you can start to ask questions about how your team can be part of that future. You get to ask, "How can I help?" This question puts you in a special category of partner. You are someone who helps customers achieve their dreams.

And that's a lot more fun than just being in the marketing department.

can influence that process is to talk to stakeholders in preparation. Make sure that anyone who contributes information, be it from your own team or other teams, is part of the process of creating the stakeholder analysis report.

CREATING MINDSHARE

When your team has completed its single page for each stakeholder group, take the report to the stakeholder contacts and get their buy-in on what has been written. This keeps you and your team grounded in reality and away from speculation. Once you've checked the results, present the final stakeholder report to your

CALCULATE THE COST OF MEETINGS

You want to have a meeting? Excellent! Let's get everyone in one room and hash out the issue. But before you have that meeting, take a moment to calculate its cost.

Most employees cost employers about $100,000 a year. This includes giving the person a desk, benefits, and salary. There are 2,000 working hours in a year (40 hours × 50 weeks), so each hour costs $50.

To figure out the cost of a one-hour meeting, multiply the number of employees by $50. If you're having a multihour meeting, multiply by the number of hours—those are really expensive.

So, now you know what it will cost to make your decision. If you have five people on your team, a one-hour meeting to discuss status costs $250 at a minimum. And ten people meeting for three hours? $1,500. This does not count the work time that's lost due to the interruption of meeting.

This isn't to say that you shouldn't have meetings. Meetings are valuable tools for getting everyone on the same page. Just make sure you're going to accomplish something worth the meeting's cost.

---

team. Get final buy-in that the report represents everyone's best understanding of what others expect from the team.

It's tempting to skip over the stakeholder step when you are rebuilding a team. After all, you know what your team is supposed to do, and your team members know it as well. Take the time to do this step anyway. If you are correct, and everyone agrees on what you need to deliver, the job will be finished quickly.

However, if you are wrong, and your stakeholders have different needs than you expected, you will be very happy that you took the time to check. Expectation mismatches are the basis of some truly nasty conflicts. Take a day or two to set expectations clearly and you'll be able to move on to your mission statement and goals with confidence.

6

Developing
a Compelling
Mission Statement

HERE'S AN INTERESTING paradox. Management books assert that a mission statement is critical to running a good organization. Yet when you ask people about mission statements, they roll their eyes and tell you that mission statements are a waste of time.

How can that be? How did one of the basic tools of leadership get such a bad reputation? Because most mission statements are useless. Why? Because they were written by well-meaning people in upper management without any input from the people they manage. The management team is excited and energized by the statement because they crafted it. They then present the statement to their company and announce it to their teams. Their teams had no involvement in crafting the statement, so it comes across as meaningless words. They read it, nod, and then go back to whatever they were doing before.

This is unfortunate, because a mission statement is critical to the success of any organization. It gives the organization clarity so that everyone has the same goals and moves in the same direction. The process of crafting a mission statement helps team members explore why they are there and what they want to accomplish.

For example, let's look at possible mission statements for an engineering organization:

+ We innovate and create new products.
+ We quickly adopt new technology and improve on it.
+ We leverage our existing products to create new products.
+ We buy innovative technology from other companies and integrate it into our product line.

These are all different missions. If the engineering team is not clear on its mission, then some of the engineers are guaranteed to be dissatisfied. The ones who believe they are there to create new products will be resentful when the company buys technology from outside. The engineers who believe they are supposed to quickly adopt new technology and improve on it will feel that the company is wasting resources trying to make its own new innovations. There will be no clear and coherent path forward.

A clear mission statement would resolve these problems. It is possible that some engineers will leave the team once they see that the team is not doing what they wanted it to do. This is OK. They can be replaced with engineers who buy into the mission; then the team will be ready to move forward together.

ELEMENTS OF A MISSION STATEMENT

The scenario just described will happen to your team if you don't have a clear mission statement. Different members of the team will have different ideas about what the team needs to do and how it should be delivered. To avoid this, it's critical that you and your team clarify your mission.

Most mission statements consist of three parts:

+ **We are:** Describes what kind of people are on this team
+ **We do:** Describes what the team provides to the company
+ **By doing:** Describes how the team does it

Here are some different mission statements that could exist for the same customer support group.

The first statement is from a team that wants to present a softer side of customer support and make all customers feel equally welcome:

> We are a focused team of customer-service professionals who provide world-class telephone support to our customers. We believe in treating our customers with the utmost respect and courtesy. As team members working toward a common goal, we support each other to create a positive and fulfilling work environment.

This next statement is for a group that is measured primarily on the profit they generate for the company. It's possible that the same team of people who prepared the previous statement would create this one if they were working in a different organization:

> We are a profit-generating center for our company. We sell service to customers and deliver a great value for the products and services they purchase. We take personal ownership of customer issues and carry them through to completion.

The next statement could also be created by the same people, but in a different context. In this case the team is a highly specialized group of technical support staff that must use its resources efficiently to meet goals:

> We are highly technical customer-support professionals. We prioritize customer support based on our customers' value to the company. We use a repeatable business system to provide a consistently high level of service.

These three statements describe customer-support departments that function in different ways and within different parameters. Each of these teams would attract different kinds of people and provide a different kind of customer experience. Imagine the chaos that would erupt if one team had different people following each of these three missions. There would be friction and hard feelings as each group became convinced that the others were doing their jobs incorrectly. That is why a clear mission is critical.

LEADING A TEAM THROUGH MISSION CREATION

When you tell most people that your team is going to create a mission statement, they picture an all-day off-site with HR facilitators, flip charts, and a multimedia presentation. None of this is necessary to create a mission statement. You can create a mission statement with your team, within your company's walls, and without facilitation.

In fact, since your company has just had a layoff, it's unlikely that you have any additional time or resources to create a mission statement. Your team needs to perform at a faster, more efficient pace now that there are fewer people. You need to fix the engine while the car is driving down the road. Here's how to do it.

Creating a mission statement with your team is a three-step process:

+ **Launch.** You, as the manager, initiate the discussion. This is where you explain the objectives of writing a mission statement to your staff.
+ **Discuss.** Once your team understands the mission statement, it needs to discuss options. You don't need to have another lengthy meeting for the discussion. This can be handled in small, impromptu meetings or in hallway conversations.

✦ **Craft.** Once your team has discussed the mission statement and what it should include, you need to craft the mission statement.

Each of these three steps is discussed in detail in the following sections.

LAUNCHING THE MISSION-STATEMENT PROCESS

The launch meeting is the kickoff for the mission-statement process. It is where you teach your team about mission statements and what they can provide, which is namely a sense of cohesiveness for the group and clarity around team goals and objectives. You may have to sell the concept or process to your staff. People tend to be more cynical in a postlayoff environment, and they may see the mission-statement process as a waste of time. You need to be clear about the value you see in the mission-statement process to help them get behind the idea. You should also consider working with another manager to create a kickoff meeting. Combined meetings have several benefits:

✦ **Your team members are more likely to value the mission-statement process if they see another manager in the company embracing it.** Conversely, the other manager's team will be impressed by the fact that you are taking proactive steps to set a vision for your team and foster postlayoff collaboration.
✦ **It reduces the workload.** You can share the teaching and training responsibilities with the other manager.
✦ **More people bring more ideas to the process.** Your team may have a certain way of viewing the organization that could limit participation or ideas. Another team could add more insight and a different perspective.

Your kickoff meeting will have the following agenda.

Explain What a Mission Is and Why It Is Important

Discuss the importance of a mission with your team. Most people are unfamiliar with the idea of a working mission statement. A mission statement fulfills the requirement that people "begin with the end in mind" (as Stephen Covey put it).

If everyone has a clear idea of what the team stands for and what it is supposed to accomplish, they will make decisions that support the team's mission. If people have different ideas of what the team is supposed to do, there will be mistakes, conflicts, and inefficiencies.

Define the Need for a Newly Clarified Mission

In a postlayoff organization, your team may have different goals or fewer people to accomplish the same work. By clarifying the mission, you will make sure the team is focusing on its most important objectives. This clarification allows you to better focus your resources and thus get more work done with less.

Suggest a Structure for the Mission Statement

Mission statements can take many forms, but there is a suggested structure. Suggest to your team that its mission statement would benefit from the following format:

- **We are:** What kind of people are on this team?
- **We do:** What does the team provide to the company?
- **By doing:** How does the team do it?

Then share examples of mission statements that follow this format.

Break into Groups and Create Mission Statements

You are now ready to launch the team into creating a mission statement. Have the team break into groups of two to four people to develop mission statements and set a date for the next meeting, when your team will meet to discuss the suggested mission statements. When you create the groups, try to mix people who wouldn't normally work together. This cross-pollination will ensure that different people and their respective jobs, functions, and needs are represented.

Breaking the team into groups and giving them a specific deadline has two purposes:

1. The group members provide accountability for each other. The need to deliver a group presentation will focus the group's attention on the task at hand.
2. The group members will naturally meet to deliver their version of the mission statement. This will promote mission discussion between the group members without needing to call another meeting.

Give each group the same assignment. They are to create a group mission statement that captures the idea of who is on the group, what they do, and why. Also let the team know that discussion among the groups is OK. This should not be a competition for who writes the best mission statement; rather, it should be a collaborative process. Each group should try to get everyone's input during the mission-statement creation process.

Give the groups some basic instructions about the mission statement. For example, if your company or your division has a mission statement, distribute that statement to the groups. Let them know that this team's mission statement must fit within the larger corporate statement. Once you've created the groups, and the deadline for the next meeting has been set, your launch meeting is complete. This should take no more than one hour.

MISSION DISCUSSION WEEK

In the classic mission-statement process, the team goes off-site to work on its mission statement. The Mission Discussion Week replaces a day of intense off-site discussion with a week of on-site background discussion. The same issues will be considered; it's just that the team will have the discussion via e-mail and during lunch and hallway conversations.

Breaking the team up into groups that have a responsibility for reporting back to the department will help facilitate the discussion.

As the manager, you play a delicate role in the process. You want to make sure people talk about the mission issues. You also want to make sure you do not dominate the conversation. You want the team to feel ownership for the mission when it is done, so you need to guide the discussion with a light hand. You can encourage the discussion in several ways:

+ Send your team members an e-mail thanking them for their participation and encourage them to share thoughts about the mission statement through an e-mail thread.
+ Make the mission statement your main topic of conversation in your informal conversations with the team. Give the mission statement a lot of thought and share your thoughts with the team in a one-on-one setting.
+ Avoid sending the team e-mails containing your thoughts about the mission statement. Such a published declaration of your preferences will squelch the debate. Instead, read the group's e-mail without responding and watch what people are saying. Use that information in private conversations with team members.

The bottom line is that you must show enthusiasm and interest in the creation of the mission statement. If you are excited by the process, people on your team will be as well.

CRAFTING A MISSION STATEMENT

Once the team has discussed the mission statement, it's time for the smaller groups to present their mission-statement ideas to the team. At this point, do a little strategy switch with your team. Instead of having the groups present their own mission-statement idea to the team, have each group present the results from one of the other teams. For example, if you have groups A, B, and C, have A give C's presentation, have B give A's presentation, and have C give B's presentation.

Doing this will reduce the tendency for people to treat this meeting as a competition. Normally, each group would try to have its own mission statement adopted. By having the groups present the mission statements of other groups, you'll discourage any sense of individual ownership and reinforce the idea that this is a team exercise.

The smaller groups will need time to learn each other's presentations. Set up two sessions in the meeting. Each group should teach its presentation in one session and learn about another group's presentation in the other session.

Now you are ready to have the groups present the ideas. There are two parts of this process:

+ **Informational presentation.** Each group presents the mission statement so that the other team members understand it. This part of the presentation is for information only. Questions can only be clarifying questions to clear up definitions or other informational questions. There is no debate in this step.
+ **Debate.** Once the missions are up on flip charts and understood by everyone, it is time to debate the wording of the mission and how the mission relates to what the team does.

You are the facilitator in this process. You may inject your opinion here and there and add information to the discussion, but you should focus on making sure the team is effectively addressing the issue. Focus on the following roles:

+ **Enforce the rules.** Make sure the people on the team follow the rules of the discussion. For example, remind people that the first part of the process allows only clarifying questions, not debate. Also, don't allow side conversations, and keep the team from digging into tangential issues that don't serve the process.

- **Include people.** If you see someone who has not spoken, ask for that person's opinion. Watch for people whose body language indicates disagreement but who don't say anything.
- **Help people understand.** During the debate, help each side understand where the other person is coming from. Make sure everyone understands everyone else's position, even if they don't agree with it.
- **Reflect agreements back to the team.** When the team agrees on a point, restate the agreement and write it down. Beware of nailing portions of the mission statement down and making them unchangeable in later discussions. This could lead to a negotiation that gets deadlocked on one issue. Instead, leave everything firmed up but open to change so people have room to maneuver.

If this process brings the team to agreement, you are finished! Get agreement on the final wording of the mission statement and publish it. If there are issues that are unresolved at the end of the meeting time, leave those issues open for further discussion during the week. Schedule a follow-up meeting. You should make it a goal to have consensus on the team. It is counterproductive to have a mission statement that people do not buy into.

Don't be afraid of the debate that may ensue. It may seem that the issues being debated have little relevance or are wording arguments. They are more than this. People are discussing the meaning of their work and their place in the organization. If you let this discussion take place, it will create a deeper sense of commitment when the mission statement is finally done.

When you do publish a mission, make a single PowerPoint slide with the mission on it and send it to your team. Print a copy for yourself and post it prominently on your wall. Use your example to demonstrate the statement's importance to your team.

Once you've reached this goal, congratulate yourself. You've taken a significant step toward revitalizing your team. You've taken a group of people who might be depressed about a disruptive layoff and given them meaning for the future. That is a great day's work!

FOCUS ON YOUR CUSTOMER'S PROBLEM

When you are prioritizing your team's time, there is a simple formula that will always give you the right answer: focus on your customer's problem. The customer could be the end customer of your company or an internal group that needs your output, but if you focus on the customer's problem you will know you are doing the right thing.

This is the value of creating the stakeholder diagram. It gives you the opportunity not only to identify your customer but also to go to that customer and make sure you are identifying what that customer needs from you and your team.

The best way to do this is to ask your customers what they need. For example, once, when I was on a software marketing team, I needed to create a presentation for the sales force to teach them about my product.

Rather than try to develop the presentation myself, I went to the best sales guy in the company and asked him, "What should I put in this presentation?" He told me he needed to know the problem the product solved, what this problem cost our customers, and who had successfully used the product in the past. I put those three things into my presentation, and the presentation was a complete success.

Clearly identify your customers and understand their problems. Once you do that, your priorities will become obvious and your customers will love you.

DEFINING GOALS

ONCE YOUR TEAM has defined its mission statement, you can move on to establishing goals. Although goals are always important, they are especially critical in a postlayoff environment. Goals focus a team and keep everyone doing tasks that relate to the mission. With the reduced head count common after a layoff, you need the team to be laser-focused on your deliverables. The mission statement is a first step; now the goals will make it real.

Goals are the deliverables your team commits to for its customers and the company. Create goals that are clear and easily measurable. People must be able to tell whether they have met a goal or whether they are off track.

Hold a meeting with your team to translate the mission you've created into goals. As with creating a mission statement, your team must be part of the goal-creation process. If you simply hand the goals to your team, you are unlikely to garner mindshare for them. If the team members do not buy in to the achievability of the goals, they are less likely to put forth as much effort. Sometimes you will be handed a goal by upper management and told to implement it. In this case you need to explain the situation to the team and take the goal as a given.

In the goal-creation meeting, you will work together to create and publish up to five goals for the team. Do not exceed five goals, because you will spread the team too thin. Think about it in terms of days. With five goals, you could give each goal an even percentage of the team's time—20 percent, or one day a week. A team with more than five goals will dilute its effort so much that it will not deliver on any of them.

Prepare for the meeting by asking the groups who created the mission statements to reconvene to create goals that will implement the mission. Before you start the goal-creation process, take the time to teach the team how to create solid goals.

CREATING SOLID GOALS

Solid goals give people a clear picture of what needs to be accomplished and when it needs to happen. Your team will be able to use solid goals to make implementation plans and to measure their progress. Clearly defined goals are easy to measure and imagine. Poorly defined goals are fuzzy, and you can't tell when you've achieved them.

Here are a few examples of poorly defined goals:

+ **Provide great customer support.** This goal sounds excellent; however, nobody can tell if it's been achieved. How is the customer support measured? When does it need to happen?
+ **Hire the best people.** Again, how do you measure this, and when does it need to happen?
+ **Support our salespeople.** How will you know if they feel supported?

These are general statements that can go into a mission statement, but they make poor goals. Make sure your goals will drive activity by using the SMART model described in the next section.

SMART Model

The SMART model is an easy-to-remember system for defining goals. This system creates five parts for each goal. When you fill in all the parts, you'll have a clearly defined goal that you can measure. There are five parts to the SMART model:

- **Specific.** The goal must have a mechanism that shows whether the specific objective has been achieved. You can make our example goal measurable by changing "Write a report . . ." to "Deliver a comparison report on IT vendors to the team." Now you have a way of measuring whether the project is complete.
- **Measurable.** You can clearly see when a specifically defined goal has been reached. For example, "Investigate IT vendors" is not specific. "Write a report comparing IT vendors" is specific. You'll know whether the report has been delivered; it is a quantifiable measurement.
- **Achievable.** The people who are assigned to the goal must believe it's feasible. If people don't believe the goal can be completed, they will not commit to it. Consult with your team members as to whether they believe the goal can be accomplished.
- **Relevant.** The goal must be tied directly to the mission. For example, a sales team that is creating a report to evaluate IT vendors is probably creating an irrelevant goal.
- **Time-bounded.** The specific, measurable result must be delivered by a certain date. Goals without dates are dreams. In our example, the goal should read, "Deliver a report comparing IT vendors to the team by May 28." That fixes the goal in time.

Your goals will be easy to write and understand once you've gotten into the habit of using the SMART model. Review the following sample goals to see how they are specific, measurable, achievable, relevant, and time-bounded.

- Meet or exceed our sales targets this year.
- Score ratings of good or great in at least 90 percent of our customer surveys by the end of Q2.

- Create sales materials that the sales forces rates as good or very good by the end of Q2. Create the necessary surveys to implement this goal.

CREATE CLEARLY DEFINED ROLES

A friend of mine once had to mediate a dispute that had split the members of his church. The issue was not one of belief or dogma. It was not about the direction of the church, or the efficacy of its outreach programs, or its stand on controversial policies. It was far tougher than any of these: it was about roles and goals.

The problem was that one of the church members had become part of the church's school committee. He was convinced that his role was to guide the pastor in choosing the curriculum, to help create the syllabus, and to act as the pastor's manager and conduit to the church's board.

The pastor thought that the school committee member's role was to supply snacks.

This question of roles and goals led to a split in the church leadership, with folks siding with either the pastor or the school committee member. It was up to my friend to mediate the split with a small group of board members who had not gotten embroiled in the mess.

They solved the problem by interviewing different members of the church to learn the traditional role of the school committee (it was to supply snacks) and the way that the various groups saw the roles that existed today and were needed.

In the end they published a document that clearly defined the roles of the school committee (policymaking, communication to the board . . . and snacks) and the pastor (spiritual leadership for the curriculum) and recommended a new administrative role of school principal, since it was obvious that the pastor was stretched too thin.

Conflicts like this, where people are not sure of their roles, can be divisive and loud. They get to the core of what people think needs to be done and what people think they can do. They are very personal battles.

These conflicts are especially common after a layoff, because all the old roles have been thrown up in the air and people are scrambling to pick up the pieces, and perhaps advance their careers.

Clarity is the key to solving these problems. Watch for conflicts that may be role-related and then help the team members clarify who needs to do what to get the job done.

Once your team has created up to five SMART goals, publish the goals on a single sheet of paper. Encourage people to keep these goals in plain sight, such as on a bulletin board, and refer to them as they execute their daily responsibilities. The goals will become the fuel that drives your execution engine later in the process.

Bring Your Stakeholders on Board

Make sure your goals are consistent with the expectations of your stakeholders. Go to the primary contacts from your stakeholder report and discuss your team's goals with each of them. Discuss disconnects early in the process and fix them.

When organizations have a layoff or restructuring, the entire organization will oscillate for a while until it finds a new equilibrium. Don't be surprised if your stakeholders change their needs after you've created your mission and goals. This is part of the reorganizing process. Eventually these changes will settle down, and you'll be able to focus on a single set of goals.

Be Seen as a Team Player

As you work on collaboration within your team of employees, make sure you are collaborating with your peers as well. It's likely that the others who report to your manager have similar missions and goals. Team players look beyond their team and share information with management peers. Make sure your team's challenge matches the challenges and goals of similar groups in your company.

For example, if your team defines one of its goals as "Increase new business growth in my department by 25 percent by Q4," you should make sure your peers are also in agreement with this number or result. Otherwise, you may be out of sync with the message

WORK WITH YOUR FELLOW MANAGERS

Middle managers can be an odd group of people. Faced with hard times and layoffs, they instinctively tend to look at their fellow middle managers as competition. The other managers can be competition for people, budget, jobs, and promotions. On the other hand, they can also be allies. They have the same job as you, they have the same problems as you—but they might have some different ideas.

Make an effort to build relationships with your peers. Like all relationships, this one will be built on your emotional bank account with your fellow manager. That emotional bank account may start out in deficit if the other manager views you as a competitor, so start making deposits early and often.

As in all new relationships, your fellow manager wants to know who you are, where you are going, and whether you can be trusted. Get those things out of the way right up front; be straightforward about your goals. Explain why you think you managers need to stick together.

Not everyone is going to share your views of collaboration; manager-to-manager suspicion runs deep. That's OK. Ignore the ones who won't work with you and find a couple who will. Now that you've got some allies, you'll be in a better position to bounce ideas off each other and influence your organization.

Make a few friends among your peers and see how quickly you feel good about your coworkers.

your peers are giving their people, or other departments may not have the resources to handle the new business your team is trying to generate.

I remember a time when I was one of several sales engineering managers. My company had a big conference each year, with a policy that all employees needed to share rooms. However, I was the only manager enforcing the policy. All the other managers were allowing exceptions to this rule.

When we discussed this in a meeting, we managers discovered that almost nobody was sharing rooms. We agreed to enforce a consistent policy across our groups. I was happy, because I didn't want to be the only manager forcing his team to follow the policy.

In the best scenario, your manager has created an environment of collaboration with your peers. You'll know what your mission and goals are and can work with your peers and your team to develop goals that make the most sense.

In a less-than-perfect world, you'll need to take a leadership role and help your peers define a common mission or set of goals so that your team is working in sync with other teams.

Influencing Remote Employees

CREATING A CLEAR challenge for your team is critical to rebuilding after a layoff and is doubly important if your team is remote. Leading collocated teams is like guiding a single scout troop through the woods. It's easy to get everyone to the same place because they can keep each other in sight. They may wind up in the wrong place, but they'll wind up there together.

Working with a remote team is like trying to get two scout troops to meet at a given location. They can't see each other, and they are coming to the location from different directions, so they need a common map and a compass to get to the spot. They will get lost without those tools.

Your team's mission statement and its goals act like the map and the compass. The mission statement is the map (it gives the team the target), and the goals are the compass (they tell the team when it's off course). This works only if everyone on your team has the same map and compass. It's your job to help the team create these tools.

The difficulty with remote teams is that the challenge-creation process is more one of influence than one of listening. Today's employees are leery of creating mission statements and other alignment activities. They've lived through too many mission-statement exercises that result in a piece of paper hanging, ignored, on a wall while the company continues with business as usual.

Your job in the challenge process is to convince your team of the process's value and to influence your team members to really engage in the process rather than simply to run through the motions so they can get back to work—regardless of whether that work is in the right direction.

The most difficult part of managing a remote team is avoiding the breakdowns and flare-ups that can occur easily in low-communication environments. The second most difficult part is influencing people who can ignore you the moment the phone call disconnects. This process moves much more slowly than the process of influencing people locally.

REMOTE COMMUNICATION

Influencing people remotely is difficult for a manager at any level and is especially difficult for a frontline manager working with a new team after a layoff. The process is like walking a tightrope. You are balanced between being completely ignored on the one side and creating communication breakdowns and hurt feelings on the other. And as with a tightrope walk, it is very difficult to negotiate the middle.

It is possible to create a safety net that will catch you if you fall. This net is the emotional bank account that you've built with your remote team members. If your team members know you, trust you, and believe that you have their best interests at heart, they will be willing to cut you some slack. If they believe in you, and believe that you know how to make their lives better, they will follow your lead eagerly.

That said, it is a drain on the emotional bank account if you are not skillful about influencing remote team members. This is especially true when you are creating a new relationship with these team members because of a sudden reorganization. If their favorite

SHOW SLIDES TO REMOTE MEETING MEMBERS

There is nothing more annoying than to sit in a presentation where someone is on a speakerphone and keeps saying, "Next slide." Well, one thing is more annoying, and that's having your printed slide look like a jumble because the presenter chose to use clever animation. If this is annoying to you, imagine how annoying it must be to your distributed team.

Presentations are an opportunity to transfer your emotions about a project to your team. If you are excited enough about the information to put together a presentation on it, you should give your team members every opportunity to view it. It's times like this when you need Web presentation software.

Once upon a time there were only two Web collaboration tools: Microsoft Netmeeting and Webex. Today we have dozens of tools, and many of them are free. Take the time to learn how to use one of these and take advantage of it the next time you need to give your team a presentation.

manager was just let go, and you are the new boss, you're going to have to work hard to gain their trust.

Influencing remote people is not easy, but it is possible. The first thing to accept is that it is a much slower process than influencing people who are in your office. You'll have to work with channels of communication that are less efficient but more effective. They will take longer to use but will save time in the long run.

Beware the Dangers of E-Mail, IM, Forums, and Other Technological Minefields

When you find yourself sitting down to write an e-mail that will convince anyone of anything, stop! Raise your hands in the air, step away from the keyboard, and nobody will get hurt.

Never, never, never try to write an e-mail that will convince other people of something, because e-mail is not a tool of influence. Trying to use e-mail to influence other people is like trying to use a hammer to cut down a tree. You might be able to do it, but you are more likely to simply injure yourself.

E-mail is useful for two things:

1. Asking a question
2. Providing information

Using it for anything else, such as convincing your team that creating a mission statement will help them be more effective, is a waste of time. If you don't believe me, just look at e-mail's cousin, the online forum. You may have had the opportunity to watch folks argue on an online forum (if you haven't, go over to the *Huffington Post* and read the comments section of a controversial article). You'll notice that people go back and forth incessantly but never agree.

Many things can go wrong when you try to influence people with e-mail, forums, IM, or other technological means of communication. These include the fact that the written word is rarely convincing. Direct-mail marketing pieces expect a 2 percent response rate; this means that these well-crafted pieces of influence have a 98 percent failure rate! Can you afford a 98 percent failure rate when you're influencing your team? No.

There is another problem with trying to influence people with e-mail: the Declaration of Independence effect. It is the fact that people become very attached to ideas once they publicly write the idea down and sign their name to it. Ask John Hancock.

What happens when we communicate an opinion by e-mail? We write the opinion down in a document with our names on it. Now we've gone public, and now we cannot change our minds. That would require a public admission that we were wrong.

This is especially true when the e-mail discussion has a large distribution list or the conversation is happening on a public forum. People often dig in their heels and stick to their guns if they think that changing their minds will cause them to lose face.

Influence by Phone; Follow Up by E-Mail

Consider the following attempts for a fictitious manager named Pat to influence a fictitious employee named Chris. First, we'll see how the exchange goes with e-mail.

From: Pat
To: Chris
Subject: Mission Statement

Hi Chris,
I'm glad we had a chance to talk last week. Now that we'll be working together I just wanted to start the process of gathering data for our mission statement. What does your schedule look like for next week?
Pat

From: Chris
To: Pat
Subject: RE: Mission Statement

I'd love to work on the mission statement, but I don't have time next week. I'm just too busy since they let Dana go. You folks can work on the statement and then just send it to me, OK?
Chris

Well, that went poorly. Pat is going to have to spend some time talking Chris back from her statement that she doesn't have the time to work on the mission statement. An even worse response would be to reply to Chris's e-mail to try to talk her into the process. This would have been handled much better as a phone call:

Pat: "Hi, Chris. You got a minute?"

Chris: "Sure."

Pat: "I've started talking to folks about how we'll gather information to start our mission statement next week, and I wanted to check your schedule."

Chris: "Oh, Pat, I don't know. I'm so busy since they axed Dana. Can't you folks work on it without me?"

Pat: "I know what you mean. We're all stressing now. I want to use the mission statement to help us get some stuff off our plates, but I need input from everyone so that we remove the right tasks. I could really use your help on this. . . . "

Now that Pat and Chris are talking, there is enough communication bandwidth for them to agree on how much Chris can contribute to the effort.

Notice also that it is much more difficult to say no over the phone than through e-mail. Chris can feel how important this is to Pat and doesn't want to come right out and say she won't help. This gives Pat the opportunity to respond to Chris's objections and put the effort into terms that are important to Chris.

Once the conversation is over, Pat can send Chris an e-mail confirming the conversation and the actions that both of them took away from the call. Now e-mail is being used as a factual tool rather than an influencing tool, and that's where it shines.

Make a Site Visit

The best way to influence a remote group is to stop being remote. Flying out and visiting a team or person gives you a burst of high-bandwidth communication that you can build on in future communication.

You physically visit a team for one reason (and it's not to be a seagull); you visit to build trust and grow the emotional bank account. Trust is the foundation of all influence. That makes trust building your highest priority. If you fly away from a site visit with a team with lots of value in everyone's emotional bank account, you will have gone more than halfway toward influencing them by phone later.

When you visit a team, be sure to create a special event to make the trip memorable. It doesn't have to be flashy—it can just be a nice dinner—but it needs to demonstrate that you put some effort into thinking about the event and that you cared enough to make it special.

The event-building process is especially important if you have your team members fly to meet you. This is a much better use of time since not only do the team members build a relationship with you but they also build relationships with each other. In these cases the special events become bonding experiences.

I once created a special event for my team when I managed a group that was almost entirely remote, with only one team member also living in Boston. I had invited everyone to Boston for a training class, so I created a fun event.

We had a good day of training, and then I took the team to the city. We went to Faneuil Hall for dinner, walked over to the Boston Garden to see a hockey game, and then walked from the Boston Garden through Back Bay.

Almost ten years later I was talking to one of those folks who brought up that event. He reminded me of the dinner and the hockey game. He also remembered the topics we had for training that day, almost a decade later. The key to that success was planning a simple event and showing that I cared enough to make their trip enjoyable.

You need to build similar experiences for your remote teams. If you can't bring them to you, then make sure that you have some fun with them when you fly out to visit. Again, your primary goal in the visit is to build trust by making deposits in the emotional bank account. Once you've built that trust, you'll find influence to be much easier.

Find a Champion

One of the most difficult business jobs is that of business-to-business selling. If you are in business-to-business sales, you are challenged both by low-bandwidth communication and by the inherent low trust that comes with being from another company.

Because of this low-trust situation, business-to-business salespeople have learned to cultivate a relationship with a person in the customer company who likes the solution and wants them to succeed. This person is called their *champion*. The champion helps the sales team get appointments, sticks up for them in internal meetings, and argues for their solution.

You need to adopt this approach when you are influencing a remote team. While you want to build trust with all your team

HELP YOUR TEAM MEMBERS EMBRACE THEIR POWER

Being an individual contributor in an organization is tough on the ego. Your time is controlled by others; the strategy of the company is controlled by others; your money is controlled by others. You are the front line to the customers, the source of all productivity, and often underappreciated.

Given the state of an individual contributor's life, it's not surprising to see that many folks on a team will fall into a state of helplessness. With each new challenge, setback, or workload increase, these folks shrug and mutter under their breath. They figure there's nothing they can do about the problem, so they shouldn't get all worked up.

Yet feeling powerless as an individual contributor is more of a decision than an accurate reflection of the state of things. When team members focus on the things they can control, they find there is a long list to work with. They can decide whether they will team up or compete. They can decide whether they will participate in the group decision-making

process. They can even decide whether they will get into work a few minutes early and have a smile on their faces.

They can also decide to find better ways to do their jobs and to lobby the management to make the changes necessary to do a better job. They can find efficiencies, snuff out waste, and participate in managing lists of group-level activities.

On a personal level, they can choose a way to organize their tasks. They can develop new skills through outside reading and work. They can decide whether to mutter about you under their breath or, conversely, to praise you when you're not in the room (or the state or country). All these things are in their control.

As the team leader it's your job to help your team see their power and see their options. Help them see what they can control and help them organize themselves to control it. If you help your team members feel in control, you will get a happier team, some great ideas, and a more enjoyable workplace.

members, you should take note if one of them resonates especially well with your effort to build a mission statement. This person is your *champion*.

It is essential that your relationship with your champion be informal. You don't want to say, "Well, Bob here agrees with me, and so Bob is in charge." This will make life difficult for you and Bob. Instead, you want to give Bob an occasional phone call to get a feeling for where the group is going and what objections are being raised. You want to learn how your ideas are being received.

Your goal in identifying a champion is to recognize that you are not alone in influencing your group. There are others who agree with you and who will help you. Once you have one person bought into the process, you can work with that person and the team to bring others into the process. Eventually, you'll get the whole team on board.

You can influence your remote teams by building trust, communicating carefully, and working with local champions. Consciously working to build consensus and influence will allow your teams to work together smoothly, no matter where they are located.

3

DEFINING ROLES
AND
MAKING A PLAN

n this section, I am assuming you cannot hire people because you've just had a layoff. This may not be the case, however. In my career I've encountered companies that let people look for work within the company after a layoff, and you may be in the same situation.

Whether you have the ability to hire or not, the steps remain the same. You are going to define the roles on your team and put people into the roles where they are most likely to succeed. Again, each task in the following chart should be completed by the Friday of the week listed.

Here are the goals for choosing:

CHOOSE

DELIVERABLE	DESCRIPTION	DATE
Assign people to roles.	Find the best matches between your team members and the available roles (see Chapter 9). Work with team members to assign them roles that suit them.	Week 8
Publish a team plan.	Work with the team to define the projects, tasks, and feedback system that will implement the team's goals (see Chapter 10).	Week 9

Having been born and bred in New England, I am a Patriots fan. There was a time when being a Patriots fan meant cheering for a perennial loser. My team was called "the Patsies," and there were those of us who wore bags over our heads at the game. Then Robert Kraft bought the team, and after a couple of false starts with coaches he found the right man for the job in Bill Belichick.

The Patriots have won three Super Bowls since Belichick came on board and became the only team in history to go 16–0. But even more impressive was the year after the 16–0 season when star quarterback Tom Brady was injured in the first quarter of the first game and the team still managed to win 11 games.

The secret to Belichick's and the Patriots' success has never been an abundance of star players. The Patriots have the same salary cap as everyone else. The secret to the Patriots' success is that Bill Belichick finds good players and uses them in a way that maximizes their talents.

The secret to Robert Kraft's success with the Patriots is that he chose Bill Belichick, a football genius, to run the Patriots. In both cases, choosing the right person for the job led to tremendous success.

Now it's your turn. You have a team, and you have the opportunity to choose good players and put them in a position to win. You have access to the same tools that Belichick and Kraft used when they turned the Patriots around. The following chapters will help you with this step:

+ Choosing people and roles
+ Creating a team plan

Let's see how to build a great team.

CHOOSING PEOPLE
AND ROLES

PUTTING THE RIGHT person in the right job is one of the rewarding aspects of management. You get the satisfaction of seeing an employee excel. The individual performs effortlessly, is easy to coach, and has higher productivity than anyone else doing the job.

Conversely, putting the wrong person in the wrong job is painful to watch. You can coach him and try to help, but you'll never get great results. It's like using a Clydesdale as a racehorse. You can train him, coach him, and feed him all the right foods, but he'll never win a race. You need to put people in a position to win by building on their innate talents and strengths.

In 1999, the Gallup Organization published the results of a study it did on workplace performance involving more than 100,000 employees of 2,500 companies. Gallup surveyed teams of varying strengths and the managers who ran them. It published and analyzed the surprising results in a book called *First, Break All the Rules*. The book presented new tools for managers that changed many people's basic way of looking at the management role.

The most powerful new tool was a survey that indicated whether an organization had hired and retained high-performing individuals. Employees responded that they agreed or disagreed with a series of statements. People in strong organizations agreed strongly with most of the statements.

Gallup ordered the statements in terms of importance. The first statement had the highest correlation to a high-performing team; the second had a lower correlation, and so on. The first six statements were essential to high-performing teams, and managers needed to make sure they were getting agreement on these before working on the next six.

The first statement in the survey supported current management understanding of what it took to create a high-performing team: *I know what is expected of me at work.*

The second survey statement reinforced the importance of finding the resources the team needed to succeed: *I have the materials and equipment I need to do my work correctly.*

However, the third statement is a bit of a surprise, and it jumps to the heart of the skill of choosing the right people for the job: *I have the opportunity to do what I do best every day.*

What a challenging statement! To answer "Strongly Agree," employees must do what they do best every day. How many of us have had jobs in which we got to do what we do best every day? Some of us get to do what we do best once in a while, or every week, but not every day. In fact, some of us never get to do what we do best.

This is why world-class performance is so rare. To stay ahead of the competition, you need to have people doing what they do best every single day.

Great managers hire people with a talent for the job. If they cannot hire people with the right talents, they try to put people into the best places to win. Great managers also treat people with different talents differently. They don't ask everyone to do the same job. They ask everyone to do the job that suits him or her. To understand how to do this well, you need to understand the difference between talents and skills.

Interviewing is a critical step in the hiring process, yet few of us have a plan for finding out whether an applicant has the talents we need for the job. Sitting around with an applicant and talking about her résumé is not the way to get the information you need to make a good hiring decision. You need to understand the person's talents, and you can get to that information only by using behavioral interviewing.

In behavioral interviewing, we ask the candidate to tell us about real times when the candidate has had to use the talent we need. Or we ask the candidate a question that tells us how often the candidate thinks about the skill we need.

For example, say you are hiring a customer-support representative. You could ask the person, "What do you think about customer support?" You'll get a generic response about how important it is to a company's success. This is useless. Instead, consider this question and

try answering it yourself: "Tell me about a time you received fantastic customer support."

How did you do? Did you immediately come up with a story? Was it full of detail? If you did, then you are probably someone who thinks about customer support and appreciates it. You are probably the type of person who would enjoy providing it to other people.

In our interview, a person who really values customer support will immediately have a story and will be able to tell it with enthusiasm and in detail. This is the person you want on your customer support team.

Work with the applicant to pull out details. You want to know exactly how this person responded to that situation in the past. This will give you a good feeling for how the person will respond in the future.

Behavioral interviewing is the key to finding the right person for the job.

KNOW THE DIFFERENCE BETWEEN TALENTS AND SKILLS

In the move *Amadeus*, we see a classic example of the difference between talents and skills. The movie highlights the rivalry between two composers. Antonio Salieri is a skillful composer in Vienna whose work is good and the result of effort. Wolfgang Mozart is a genius whose work springs from training combined with his innate brilliance.

Mozart was able to write incomparable music with apparently little effort. In the movie, Salieri, driven mad by his own mediocrity, makes the mistake of comparing himself to Mozart and eventually kills Mozart out of jealousy. The question is this. If you were hiring a team of composers to create a critical piece of music, whom would you want on your team—Mozart or Salieri? Naturally, you would want Mozart (assuming you could deal with his personality). In fact, you would take all the Mozarts you could get.

Do such obvious talent differences exist in business? Most managers have been trained to say no. They have been taught to believe that anyone can do any job with the right coaching and training. Many employee-development programs perpetuate this idea through competency models that attempt to describe the behavior of excellent employees. These models imply that you can make any employee into a great performer by highlighting behavioral weaknesses and improving them through training and coaching.

This is the wrong approach. Innate talents made Mozart a much better composer than Salieri, despite Salieri's training and attempts to improve. Innate talents will make Employee A much better than Employee B. It won't matter what kinds of books or classes Employee B uses. Employee A will always be better if Employee A has more talent.

The authors of *First, Break All the Rules* found startling differences in productivity between talented people and average people. For example, great customer-service reps can solve the same customer problem with one-third the number of phone calls. Engineering managers know that great software engineers create code ten times faster than average software engineers.

How is this possible? Why is it that one person can habitually outperform another? The first part of this answer lies in the definition of a talent. In *First, Break All the Rules*, Buckingham and Coffman defined a talent: "A talent is a recurring pattern of thought, feeling, or behavior that can be productively applied."

Talents start forming when we are young. They originate from the way our brain wires itself in response to the overabundance of information we receive. Soon after we are born, our brains form billions of connections between our neurons, called *synapses*. These synapses channel every piece of information we receive from the world around us into our minds and memory.

However, it's impossible to handle every piece of information. There is simply too much, and we'd be immobilized with data. The brain begins to solve this problem at about age three. From the age of three to about thirteen, the brain begins closing some synaptic pathways and strengthening others. The pathways that get used most frequently get stronger, and the ones that get used rarely become weaker. This process continues well into the teenage years.

By the time we are adults, our brain has developed an effective filter to help us handle all the data in our lives. The parts of our brains that grew stronger during development create fast, high-bandwidth connections for certain kinds of information. The parts of our brain that died away due to lack of use form slow, cans-on-a-string kinds of connections. The result is a filter that affects what we see in the world.

This filter creates our talents. Someone who notices what people wear and is drawn to the patterns, colors, and trends in clothing will have a talent for buying clothes. This person will naturally do the things necessary to succeed in the clothing industry and may easily become an excellent designer or buyer for a department store.

When you assign someone to a role, your decision should be based on talent rather than experience or skill. The person who has a talent for a role will always outperform someone without the talent who has to work at the skills. You'll usually find considerable overlap between talents and skills. This is because people tend to enjoy using their talents, and the practice creates great skills. The key is to hire people based on their innate abilities rather than lines on a résumé.

When you are creating roles on your team, you must take your employees' innate talents into account. This is particularly critical after a layoff, as you probably have fewer people than before or more work and the same number of people. After a layoff, your organization is struggling to reestablish itself with its customers, vendors, stockholders, and the marketplace. You cannot afford to spend your time jamming square pegs into round holes.

CREATING THE RIGHT ROLES FOR YOUR TEAM

Teams work best when people have well-defined roles that fit together to deliver a result. Usually these roles exist as part of the historical structure of the organization. However, after a layoff you may have the opportunity to create the roles that best deliver the results from your team. Even if you don't have the opportunity to create new roles, creating the ideal organization can help you find holes in the way you are currently delivering services.

Examine the Work Flow

To create roles on your team, start by looking at the work flow. Examine three things:

- **Inputs.** How does your team get the inputs it uses to create its outputs?
- **Work process.** What does your team do to the inputs to create the outputs?
- **Outputs.** How does your team deliver its outputs and measure the results?

When you answer these questions, you'll have a clear idea of the roles on your team. You can develop an optimal work flow by creating roles that convert inputs to outputs most efficiently.

For example, I once worked with a group of customer-support engineers who answered the phone when customers called for help. The customers loved getting an engineer on the line because they got help more quickly. But the engineers disliked this arrangement because the phone calls made it difficult to work on projects that required concentration. They disliked being tied to a phone for blocks of time each day.

We solved the problem by creating a new role, a customer-service specialist who answered the phones and assigned the questions to the engineers. This was a more efficient system because we could pay administrative wages for phone answering and engineering wages for engineering work. This was a case in which creating new roles solved the problem.

Start with the Optimal Organizational Structure

Always start the role-creation process by creating an organizational structure that best delivers your team's goals and then modify that organization to match the talents and needs of your employees. Starting with an optimal organization has several advantages:

- It gives you a clear picture of the optimal team for later hiring.
- It shows you where you need to make the greatest compromises with your current team.
- It keeps you from chasing your tail trying to fit the people to the jobs and the jobs to the people. You create the best organization first, and then you adjust for the people.

Consider Taking Charge of Role Creation

The concepts of collaborative management and collaborative decision making are discussed extensively in this book. Since the roles and composition of the team are a team decision, one would expect this decision to be made as a team. Tread carefully here. This may be a decision you want to make yourself.

As teams mature, they develop the ability to handle difficult personal decisions. However, early in team development, it may be impossible for people to see beyond their individual needs when influencing a team decision. This is particularly true after a layoff, when most employees are feeling shaky about their job security.

Role creation is a difficult subject for new teams to handle because employees have a tough time looking dispassionately at the problem without taking their own skills into consideration. Team members each believe that what they do best is important, so they

HIRE FOR ATTITUDE AND APTITUDE

New hires are the raw material of your team. They bring new skills, new personality, and new energy into the group. As a manager, it's your job to help folks polish their raw materials into outstanding performance. But you can't polish a lump of coal into a diamond, and that's why you need to hire for the things you can't polish: attitude and aptitude.

Attitude speaks to the person's outlook on life. It is a reflection of the filter the person uses to understand the world. We can't change someone's attitude—heck, we can barely control our own attitudes. You're going to have to live with your new hire's attitude, so choose well. There are two things to beware of when you hire.

The first is any hint of the applicant's whining about the current job. If you ask, "Why are you looking for a new job?" you had better not hear "Because my boss is a jerk and I can't work for him."

If you hear that on an interview, when any smart person is putting on a positive show, you can be sure that when this person interviews again you will be the jerk and this person will not be able to work for you.

Second, watch out for people who generalize bad news and think of good news in the specific. This is a key sign of a bad attitude. Depressed, and depressing, people see a bad event and think of it as normal, just as they think of a good event as the exception. Optimistic people see a bad event as the exception in a world where things tend to work for you. You want optimistic people on your team. These worldviews should emerge as you interview your candidates and ask them to tell stories about their past.

As a klutz, I can't stand natural athletes. These are the folks who come into any sport that I'm playing, and regardless of how much I've practiced and how much I've sweated, they will

cannot be good resources in putting together an optimal group structure.

In a case like this, you may want to create your own set of optimal roles and discuss it with the team members one-on-one. This is also known as "socializing" an idea. You make sure that everyone on the team knows the plan before you make it public, and you handle any serious objections or oversights in private.

That way, when you present the plan publicly, you'll get a room full of people nodding their heads in agreement, rather than disbelief and anger.

be better than I am in seconds—even if they've never played before in their lives. As someone who has to sweat out every ounce of skill, I find these people maddening.

On the other hand, I want them on my side if I'm building a basketball team. They have aptitude—a natural ability to learn new skills in a certain domain. People with great aptitudes exist for software programming, sales, marketing, and customer support, as sure as they exist for physical sports. You want these people on your team.

Just as you can take a naturally great basketball player and teach her to run a pick-and-roll play, you can take a naturally great customer support person and teach her how to settle an irate client based on the client's communication style. The pick-and-roll and the settling techniques are skills, and the person with natural ability will pick them up quickly.

You can recognize people with great aptitude by looking at their résumé and talking about their past. People who rise quickly in their profession, who quickly take on more responsibility than their years would indicate, and who could talk all day long about the intricacies of the profession are people with a great aptitude for the profession.

People who never seem to get ahead, who struggle to make modest contributions, and who seem to need coaching to accomplish simple tasks do not have a great aptitude for the job. If you ask them about their past in the field and they can't remember details, you know you are missing out on aptitude.

Try as you might, you will never imbue someone with a good attitude or the right aptitude. Don't even try. Hire for attitude and aptitude and your great team will build itself.

Devise Job Descriptions

As the manager, it is your job to look at your team's mission and devise a job description or set of job descriptions that will optimally deliver the goals. You also need to collaborate with your peer managers to make sure they agree with your job description and would use a similar description for their groups.

Before you start writing a job description, you need to look at the structure of your group to understand what kinds of roles it requires. Some groups have several people who all do the same job, such as a customer-service department. Other groups have people with different jobs who complement each other. You need to clearly define each job in your group.

When you create the job descriptions you need to define four areas:

+ **Results.** What are the tangible results that you want to get from the person doing the job?
+ **Tasks.** What tasks will the person need to do to achieve the goals?
+ **Skills.** What skills does the person need to accomplish the tasks?
+ **Talents.** What underlying talents will make the person excel at the skills?

The easiest way to do this is to get a whiteboard and create a matrix like the one shown in Figure 9.1. Start at the left with results and work your way across to talents. Use your best employees as your model. Think about the talents they exhibit and how you can find more employees like them.

Figure 9.1 is a job description for a software trainer who teaches people how to use a company's software product. Here is the manager's worksheet for the role of software trainer.

Let's follow a set of results back to the talents.

+ **Results.** The trainer must receive a 90 percent approval rating from student feedback forms.
+ **Tasks.** The trainer must be able to teach ten to twenty people in a class and help them with their labs.
+ **Skills.** The trainer must be able to present effectively to a group of trainees. The trainer must also be able to interact with customers to help with labs.
+ **Talents.** The trainer must love the products and their use, be a natural communicator, and be good at public speaking.

Notice that one of the talents listed here is "love the products." This does not look like a talent at first glance, but it matches the

FIGURE 9.1

JOB DESCRIPTION TABLE FOR SOFTWARE TRAINER

Results	Tasks	Skills	Talents
Receive 90% approval rating from customers	Teach classes of 10–20 people	Present to an audience and command its attention	Loves public speaking
Teach 12 classes per month	Assist students with labs	Develop detailed product knowledge	Fascinated by our product and industry
Deliver one new class per year	Gather data from engineering for class development	Excel at software usage	Enjoys making the complex seem simple
Deliver new versions of classes to match new versions of software	Edit presentations in PowerPoint	Strong written communication	Open and likable personality
		Interact with customers and handle reports	

definition of talent given earlier. It is a habitual pattern of thought that can be used productively. So "love of the product" falls into the category of talents.

Also, notice that "public speaking" is described as a talent and that "present effectively to a group of trainees" is a skill. This is because teaching people how to use software is a skill built on the talent of public speaking. There are people who are wonderful public speakers but don't know technology or know how to teach. These people would not have the skills to do the job. However, their talent would make them good potential teachers if they received the right training.

The combination of results, tasks, skills, and talents creates the definition of a world-class trainer. This becomes the job description you will use to analyze the people on your team and compare their strengths and weaknesses.

You can share this information with your team once you've created your initial draft. They will have insights that can help you refine the description. This also gets them to start thinking about how they will fit into the team.

Evaluate Employees to Fit Them into the Optimal Team

Once you've defined the roles, it's time to evaluate your team members and see how they can fit together to make the optimal team. You use the matrix to evaluate people. You start with results and then look at talents, skills, and finally tasks (experience). This approach may be used when evaluating new candidates and for existing employees.

- **Results.** What are the exact goals that I need this employee to meet?
- **Talents.** Does this employee have the necessary talents to succeed?
- **Skills.** Does the employee have the training to do the job?
- **Tasks.** Is the employee managing tasks and time properly?

Once you've completed this analysis, you can share what you've found with the employees and develop a plan of action. This system allows you to find areas where you may be neglecting the employee in terms of training or clear direction.

PLACING PEOPLE IN THE RIGHT POSITIONS

It is unlikely that you'll have a team of employees who consistently excel at all aspects of their job. Most likely your team will have people who exhibit some, but not all, of the talents needed for their roles. Your job is to put your employees into positions where they are most likely to succeed.

For example, suppose you are running the training organization just described. You may have one employee who loves teaching and would happily teach multiple classes a month. However, this employee hates developing class curriculum. On the other hand, you may have another employee who loves developing classes but doesn't enjoy teaching or presenting in front of groups.

In this case you should not try to force both employees to deliver all the goals in the matrix. Instead, let them work to their strengths. Let the employee who loves teaching focus on that aspect of the job while the other employee develops the curriculum. You'll find that you have two highly productive employees who love their work instead of two moderately productive employees who like only part of their jobs. Knowing what talents your employees possess enables you to arrange roles to create the strongest possible team.

Once you've defined the roles for your team and believe you've found the best person for each role, it's time to get feedback from your staff. First, meet with the entire department. Explain the roles in the group and how you see the team operating. Your staff may give you some excellent feedback at this point. Rather than defend your decisions, listen during this meeting and make sure people know you understand their perspective.

Influence is a two-way street. People are influenced only by those they feel they can influence. Therefore you need to open up your thinking and modify it if you hear an idea that improves on the work you've done. If you ignore your team's feedback, you'll be viewed as another manager who doesn't listen. People will nod their heads, pretend to agree with you, and then do what they want. If you listen, you're more likely to have buy-in for your decision.

Here's an example. One sales manager had a nationwide team of sales engineers reduced as the result of a layoff. The engineers supported salespeople across North America, and because of their reduced numbers, they would need to cover for each other more than before.

The manager thought the best solution to this problem would be to combine their territories into a single North American territory. That way they could help each other and get quota credit for all the work.

Rather than simply announce the new plan to the sales engineers, this manager approached them informally over lunch and raised the idea of combining the territories. He was surprised when he got immediate pushback from his best people. They liked the feeling of personal achievement and accountability that came from having their own territories.

The manager listened to them and showed them that he was listening by describing their concerns back to them: "You're worried that one big territory will reduce your feeling of accomplishment." When they acknowledged that he had it right, he asked them, "How should we handle our reduced head count then?" The team members saw the problem and agreed they should break North America into three pieces so they could help each other and still have control over a smaller territory. The manager agreed to this approach, and they implemented it together.

If the manager had simply tried to ram the nationwide plan down their throats, they would have resisted, and it would have created tension on the team. This tension would have added to the already tense atmosphere after the layoff. The engineers might have agreed to make the plan work, but they would not have been bought in. Because this manager listened and made it clear that he could be

REQUIRE UNANIMOUS CONSENSUS ON HIRING

Everybody wants to hire the right person. You want to hire the right person so you can improve your team. Your manager wants the right person so that you won't be distracted by a performance problem, and your team members want the right person because they'll be relying on him or her.

Given all these stakeholders, you should do two things with every hire:

1. Make sure every group is represented in the interview cycle.
2. Require a unanimous consensus before you hire.

I have never—and I repeat, never—made a good hiring decision by overriding my team. Every time I've done this, it has led to a hiring mistake. Don't think you have some unique insight that everyone else has missed. Don't think you have uncovered some secret bias that's keeping someone on the committee from supporting this great candidate. Accept the fact that everyone on that committee wants the same thing and that different people notice different aspects of a person.

Hiring is a critical decision that affects everyone on your team, your customers, and your management chain. You must get hiring decisions right. Take advantage of the fact that all of us are smarter than any of us and require 100 percent consensus on hiring decisions. You'll sleep a lot better.

influenced, the team allowed itself to be influenced and created a workable solution.

BALANCING POWER SHARING AND DECISION MAKING

Throughout this book, we've discussed the need to share power and responsibility with your team. This makes the team self-reliant and allows the team members to take ownership of their work. However, when it comes to role creation you will need to balance power sharing with autocratic decision making. The level of balance is based on your team's maturity.

Different teams have different levels of decision-making ability. Some new teams that consist of people who have never experienced shared power will be unable to make meaningful decisions together at first. They won't be able to see each other's point of view or engage in a debate and will need the manager to make all but the most basic team decisions. As these teams improve in maturity, they will become able to handle more difficult issues.

For example, an immature team will have problems with open-ended decisions like "What is our mission statement?" In these cases you will need to give them multiple-choice answers and lead them by the hand through the processes we've discussed. The level of questions the team can answer will rise as you push responsibility down to them and expect them to grow.

Questions about roles and job descriptions are the most difficult questions a team faces. These questions affect people's jobs very deeply and can even affect who has the skills to remain on the team. When you ask a team to handle these kinds of issues, you run the risk of having your decision-making process degenerate into lobbying. People will argue for roles that match their talents, skills, and interests, and they will probably be unable to see the big picture.

This is understandable. People's self-esteem requires that they view their own talents as important and critical. Therefore, a person who has great communication skills will argue that the roles in the group should require great communication skills. This person's filter will accentuate the importance of these skills over others.

It is very likely that you will need to make decisions about roles on your own and as you see fit. You should talk to the team about the roles as outlined earlier, but it is unlikely that you'll please everyone or create roles that match everyone's desires. In this case, you need to work with your manager and use your own vision to craft the roles and team functions.

HIRING REMOTE EMPLOYEES

The hidden secret of all management success is hiring the right people. When you hire the right people, the rest of the job is easy. When you hire the wrong people, you set yourself up for failure. Hiring is even more critical when you are hiring a remote employee, because you won't be there to provide critical coaching.

Hiring the right employee depends on understanding the employee's environment, the needs of the job, and the employee's skill set and work habits. The environment makes a big difference as to the kind of support your employee will get and the way your employee will acclimate to the company.

Remote Environment

The remote employee's environment determines how much experience that employee will need to succeed. When we can't work next to an employee, we need someone who can accomplish things without our help. We need a self-starter and, more important, a self-corrector and self-closer. The degree of self-starting, self-correcting, and self-closing the employee needs depends on the environment.

The first question to ask about a remote employee's environment is "How remote is remote?" Is your remote employee in a different building, town, state, or country? What are the time zone considerations? Will you need to get up at 6:00 A.M. to have a phone call? Will the employee? Can you meet for lunch easily?

The closer you are to your remote employee, the easier it is to coach the person, since coaching requires that you watch the coached in action. Your communication bandwidth will also be much better if you are in the same time zone, rather than if you have a short overlap time each day.

The second question about your remote employee's environment has to do with the office. Sometimes a remote employee is working in a company office that happens to be in another place. These are the easiest situations, because an employee who is sitting in a company office will acclimate to the culture more quickly and will be able to leverage the company's resources, such as telephones, cafeterias, conference rooms, and internal Web pages.

An employee who works in an office with other members of the same company will have an easier time adjusting to the company culture. Simply being inside the firewall makes a big difference to what resources your employee can use.

The most difficult situation is one where your employee works from home. Working from home leaves people out on their own in a sort of contractor mode. They have no connection to the corporate culture, and there are no checks on the employee's behavior. An employee working from home won't have the subtle pressure to show up in the office, so it's easy for such an employee to get distracted with home issues.

Imagine the employee is sitting at home, working, and the kids get home from school. They need a ride to their friend's house, they need a snack, and they need help with their homework. Then the dog needs to go out, the yard needs to be mowed, and it's time to help with cooking supper. Then . . . oops . . . another day has gone by, and the employee has accomplished very little.

Nature of the Job

Different jobs require different levels of self-reliance. At the simple end of the spectrum, you can have a grocery bagger who works for you in another store and that person can do a fine job. Little personal initiative is needed to succeed at bagging groceries—though it helps.

On the other hand, a product marketing manager may require a significant amount of coordination with other team members, coaching, and management assistance to be effective at the job. Not to say that complexity requires more management. A business development manager has a very complex job and must be able to thrive without local management assistance, so the situation changes with the job at hand.

LOOK FOR "MORE LIKE THIS"

Back in the early days of amazon.com, the website had a button that helped you search its inventory. You'd type in a book title, and several titles would appear. You picked the title that was closest to the one you wanted and clicked a link called "More like this one."

Since then, I've used the "more like this one" approach to hiring. There are dozens of factors to consider when hiring someone for a complex job. We have to consider people's skills in many areas, their talents, their traits, and the kinds of things they enjoy doing. It's difficult to tell which of these is most important when trying to hire a great employee.

Fortunately, we have a clue about what to look for in new employees: great existing employees. When we look at our best people, we are likely to see common traits across all of them. They may all have strong technical skills or a focus on people. They may all be kind, or organized, or excellent writers.

We look at the traits in our current stars, write them down, and then click on "More like these." We use the current stars as the standards by which we judge new people for similar jobs. When we do this, we need to have a large enough pool of strong players to understand which traits are common and give them an advantage in their job and which traits are just individual to the employees. I've seen situations where my top three people were wildly different, but all shared a strong technical skill set and exuded the self-confidence of someone who had successfully done our customer's job. When I hired new people, I clicked on "more like these" and found someone who was unlike the first three in every way except for strong technical skills.

To find new stars, examine your current stars; then look for "more like these."

You need to examine the job your remote employee will be doing and connect it to the level of coaching you can provide. If the person is a few time zones away from you, you may not be able to provide much coaching, so you'll need to hire someone who can do that job without coaching. The complexity of the job will determine how much coaching you need to provide.

Employee Skill Set

The combination of the distance of your remote employee and the complexity of the job tells you how much independence you need to see in your employee before you make a hire. An employee who is doing a simple job, sitting in a nearby company office, needs a lot less competence than an employee doing a complex job working from home in another country. This section shows one way of thinking about competence and what you should look for in a remote employee.

When we talked about hiring, we looked at the talents and skill levels necessary to do the job. Now we are going to take that model to one more level to understand what level of employee competence we need when we hire. We're going to do this with the "conscious competence" model of skills, which is a good tool to use to describe the level of competence needed for a remote employee. Since different remote employee situations require different levels of skill, we need to have language to describe what we are looking for in each situation.

The model divides competence into four stages. The stages look like this, and we travel through stages following the numbers in this table. Let's look at the stages by using an example skill that many of us need to acquire: presenting to a group without saying "Um."

Here are the stages:

	COMPETENT	INCOMPETENT
Conscious	3	2
Unconscious	4	1

1. **Unconsciously Incompetent.** At first we don't even know that we are saying "um" when we give a presentation. We just go along and present. Then our manager asks us to attend a presentation skills class, and we see ourselves on the video screen saying "um," "um," "um." At that point, we have moved out of Stage 1.

2. **Consciously Incompetent.** Now we catch ourselves saying "um" all the time. It distracts us and annoys us. We give presentations, say "um," and stop talking for a moment to berate ourselves. We start learning that silence is golden and to be quiet as we think of the next thing to say. We are on to Stage 3.

3. **Consciously Competent.** We get through our first presentation without saying "um." It was a lot of work, and we had to think about it, but we made it through. We keep on presenting, and we slip sometimes, but usually we make it through. Then it begins to get easier and easier, and we stop thinking about it. We are at Stage 4.

4. **Unconsciously Competent.** It no longer occurs to us to say "um." We simply present without it. We get compliments on what fine presenters we are, and our audience doesn't notice how smoothly things went because, after all, we never say "um" when we present.

These four stages apply to all skills. They don't apply to talents, since talents are things we naturally focus on. We have no control over our talents, but we do have control over our skills. That said, we are more likely to develop unconsciously competent skills in areas where we have talents.

Unconsciously competent people are the easiest to manage from a skills perspective because they have already internalized the skills they need to succeed. The consciously competent are on the right track, because they are self-correcting. They tend to notice when they are making a mistake, and when you point out that they are using a skill wrong, they know immediately what you are talking about.

The incompetent are more difficult to work with. The consciously incompetent are usually willing to learn, but that's not a given. They may know they do a task badly and simply not care enough about the skill to improve it.

The unconsciously incompetent will probably never make it through the résumé-screening stage for your hiring process since they are unlikely to have the right jobs on their résumé to start the process.

Combining Job Conditions and Competence When Hiring

Now we can put together the location of the office and the type of work with the description of the person we need for the job. The key is to hire not only for talent but also for the right level of training given your ability to coach the new employee. We'll match the four competency levels with the job situations to which they apply.

UNCONSCIOUSLY INCOMPETENT. These people have no idea what they are doing. They are usually fresh out of college or high school and have no experience in the job or the industry. These folks are usually the least expensive folks on the market, but you can hire them only if several of the following conditions are met:

- The job needs to be easy and require little personal initiative.
- The person needs to be physically close by so that you can provide frequent coaching sessions.
- If you are not physically close by, you need to have a local team leader or another manager who will take responsibility for training this new person.
- The person needs to be working in an office environment, with a team of people to help the person understand the norms of the company.

It's best if all of these conditions are met, but you need to have at least three of them in place to have a chance of success with a person at this level of competency.

Example: You can hire someone at this level who is doing a physical job, such as cleaning or moving inventory. These jobs require very little personal skill and are easy to manage remotely. In most cases, there will be a local shift supervisor who will train the person and teach the skills.

CONSCIOUSLY INCOMPETENT. This person doesn't know how to do the job but at least recognizes the fact and is trying to improve. The only difference between hiring someone at this level and at the first level is that you don't need as much close coaching contact with this person. People at this level know their limitations and will be more likely to ask for help when they get out of their depth.

However, any level of incompetence is difficult to manage from a remote site. You still will want three of the four criteria for the unconsciously incompetent person in place.

Example: You can afford to have a retail salesperson in a cell phone store who learns on the job. The person will most likely have a feel for cell phones and the people who use them but needs to learn how to sell. This person will be upset to lose sales and will be motivated to learn if there is a local supervisor there to teach selling.

CONSCIOUSLY COMPETENT. People at this level know how to do the job, even though they have to think about it to get the job right. You can work remotely with someone at this level based on the critical-ity of the job. If you have a job that must be done right, you'll want a higher level of experience. If the job can absorb some mistakes as the person learns the ropes, you can hire someone in this category.

The consciously competent employee will have only one or two areas that need improvement and will have developed unconsciously competent skills in other areas of the job. As a remote manager you can either set up a coaching program to help this person improve or find a local person to do the job.

A person at this stage may also be able to handle working out of the home. Professionals at this level will have learned how to man-age their time and will not let themselves become distracted by a home office situation.

Example: Sales engineers need to understand complicated tech-nical tools and may know how to handle a sales meeting without damaging the prospects of a sale. But many of these folks are just

LISTEN TO THAT "LITTLE VOICE"

Hiring a new employee is one of the highest-risk decisions. In one step, you can enrich your team with a fresh face and new energy or drag yourself down into a morass of endless worrying about this person who is just not working out.

Bad employees destroy organizations. They foment dissent, pit people against one another, drop the ball, and become, in the end, just another problem. They require you to go through the sleepless nights that it will take to correct them, document them, and then, eventually, fire them.

If you hire enough people, you will eventually hire a bad one. The person will look good on paper, interview well, and have good references who will say that this person can absolutely do the job. Then the person will turn out to be terrible, despite all the good indications you had.

Given all that can go wrong, you must never, never, never hire somebody if you have misgivings. That small voice that says "Uh-oh" is always correct. Pay attention to this voice and be ready to listen to it when you are most desperate to make the hire.

I know one manager who had recently been promoted and was desperate to replace his position on the team so he could stop doing his old job and focus on management. His first move was a mistake: hiring an employee who raised a little flag during the interview process by complaining about her current manager. He spent the next six months dealing with her inability to do the job and eventually had to fire her. Not a good start.

Always listen to that little voice that says "Uh-oh." It's smarter than you think.

---

learning their sales skills and will slip sometimes. In this case you could use the local salespeople as coaches for the new sales engineer. While the job has some criticality, it can withstand a person who is just learning.

UNCONSCIOUSLY COMPETENT. This person has achieved the highest level of skill in the given profession and can operate with little or no supervision. You need someone like this when you have a very poorly defined job that requires a high level of personal initiative, combined with a home office situation where the person has nobody to watch and coach.

Example: You are hiring a business development manager to create a sales channel in Europe. You need somebody who has a proven ability to get large jobs done with no supervision. The person needs to be able to point to two or three other successes in the same field. In the case of this job, you will also want somebody with the contacts necessary to find the job.

Hiring the right person for a remote job is even more important, if that is possible, than hiring the right person for a local job. The lack of daily observation, the low communication bandwidth, and the lack of local coaching mean that this person will be at a developmental disadvantage relative to other players on the team. Therefore, you need to hire somebody who doesn't need the supervision or who is in a role that can withstand a low level of supervision.

10

CREATING
A TEAM PLAN

COMPANIES WILL ALMOST always reduce head count in a layoff without reducing the amount of work that needs to get done. This is simple economics. Layoffs are implemented to increase productivity—that is, the revenue generated per employee. If the company reduces the number of people and also reduces activity, then revenue will decrease along with head count, and productivity will remain flat.

As a result, your team will almost always be asked to do the same amount of work with fewer people. In this case you need to make sure that everyone on your team is focused on activities that will achieve the group's goals.

As a manager, you must carefully use three irreplaceable resources:

✦ **Time.** Time is not replaceable. When it's wasted, it's gone.
✦ **Talent.** You cannot easily replace people, especially after a layoff.
✦ **Attention.** People can focus on a limited number of goals. If your team is focused on the wrong goals, then it is ignoring something important.

Here is an example of an engineer who was wasting all three: A project leader in a computer company found one of her team members engaged in an odd activity. He was examining all the screen interfaces in the software to make sure the colors matched. He called this "creating a high-quality product." However, there were two problems with this activity:

+ The software under development had severe stability issues, causing it to crash constantly. Clearly, stability was a higher priority than color choices.
+ Very few of their customers owned color computer terminals at that time, so consistent colors added little value to the product.

The engineer was wasting his time on features nobody would use. He was wasting his talent because he wasn't fixing the real problems, and he was wasting his attention fixing bugs no one would see.

To make optimal use of time, talent, and management attention, you need great planning. You need to make sure that all your team members are delivering results that contribute to critical requirements. There are two reasons to do this planning with your team rather than make the plan by yourself:

+ Planning does not occur in a vacuum. Great plans benefit from multiple points of view.
+ It is impossible for the team members to feel ownership of a plan that was dictated to them. You can avoid this disconnection by including your team in the planning process.

Results in business boil down to one thing: what tasks do the people on the team accomplish each day? The key to successful planning is to link tasks to the overall goals of the team in a clear fashion. This is a difficult task if the team goals are very general.

For example, say your team's goal is "Deliver a go-to-market strategy for our spatula by June 15." Can your employees put this goal on their daily to-do list? No. The goal is too broad and doesn't lend itself to daily activity.

In this chapter, we'll discuss a system that breaks lofty goals down into individual projects and then breaks these projects down into tasks (see Figure 10.1). The planning system has four parts:

- **Goals.** These are the well-defined results that you and your team plan to deliver to your company.
- **Projects.** Complex goals usually need to be broken into several projects. Though multiple people may work on a project, only one person has ownership of each project.
- **Tasks.** These are the individual tasks, such as documents that need to be written or people who need to be contacted, that have to happen for the project to be completed. Tasks are usually done by a single owner.
- **Feedback.** Feedback is the method you use to ensure that your team is meeting its goals.

The planning process started when your team defined the goals (as described in Chapter 7). Now you and your team will create a plan that delivers those goals by breaking them into projects and then breaking those projects into individual tasks. Your feedback loop will tell you if your plan is working.

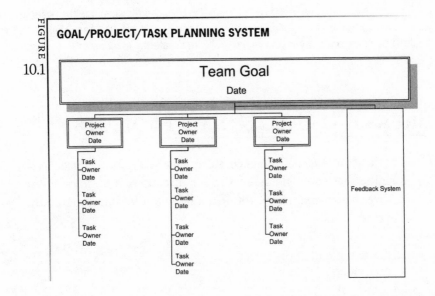

FIGURE 10.1

GOAL/PROJECT/TASK PLANNING SYSTEM

RECOGNIZE GENIUS I: MEMORY FOR DETAILS

Geniuses are all around us, and we want them on our team. Geniuses make the work look easy, they seem to succeed effortlessly, they deliver ten times the productivity of the average employee, and yet they don't seem to do any additional work. They are the key to a great team's success.

Like great players in professional sports, a genius can pick up a team and carry it across the finish line. Geniuses want the ball when the times are tough, and they deliver when given the opportunity. Your ability to recognize and hire geniuses will catapult your career and help your team recover from a layoff. The key is recognizing genius when you see it.

Watch for great memories for detail. Genius is a function of how our brains and bodies work. It comes from being fascinated by a line of work and replaying scenes from that line of work in our heads.

For example, think of a friend of yours who is a tremendous golfer. You wouldn't be surprised to hear your golfer friend say something like this when you mention the seventeenth hole of a local golf course: "I played that course last May. I think I shot a seventy-five or maybe a seventy-four. That seventeenth hole is a killer. It goes up that hill and then doglegs right—I barely parred that thing."

Your golfer genius will then go on to describe the rest of the hole in detail and can even compare it to playing that hole at other times of the year and then compare it to holes on other courses.

Geniuses can do this sort of thing because they spend their time picturing the activity in their minds and going over it repeatedly to see how they could do it better. They like doing it because the activity interests them, and this is why they are great.

When you hire, or when you evaluate talent, look for this ability to remember details from individual activities. The geniuses will be able to fill them in because they can see the event in their mind's eye. The rest of us need to re-create the memory from context.

BREAKING GOALS INTO PROJECTS

Think about the convenience store closest to your house. Now imagine that someone asked you for directions from your house to that convenience store. Your directions would sound something like this:

1. Go to the end of the street.
2. Take a left.

3. At the first traffic light, take a right.

4. The store will be on the left side of the street.

Now think about directions you'd give someone to get to another city. For example, if you wanted to give directions from Boston to New York City, you'd say the following:

1. Take Route 90 west.

2. Take Route 84 south.

3. Take Route 91 south.

4. Take Route 95 south to New York City.

Notice the difference in detail between the directions to the corner store and the directions to New York City. The directions to the corner store contain more details than the directions to New York City. They point out individual turns and landmarks and allow you to check your progress frequently. The directions to New York City tell you only highway numbers and rely on you to figure out the exit number and individual turns.

We use different levels of abstraction because people can handle only a certain range of detail. It would be confusing and impractical for someone driving to New York to have directions that described every bend and turn of the road. The same problem of abstraction applies to achieving goals. A complex goal cannot immediately be broken down into individual tasks. That would make it difficult for your staff to understand the relationships between the tasks.

Instead, goals should be broken down into projects, and projects should then be broken down into tasks. Projects provide a level of abstraction that helps people see the big picture and relate their individual tasks to the entire project.

Projects usually take more than one person to complete and indicate a higher-level step in a process. For example, say your group needs a phone script for a set of new products. Your project would be "Create a phone script for the new line of products," which supports your goal to "Meet or exceed sales goals for this year." Creating the phone script may require research, writing, testing, and review, but those items would be tasks within the project.

Be sure to use the SMART format to clearly describe projects. Each project should also have a single owner who is responsible for coordinating its completion. Once you've divided your goal into projects, you are ready to assign tasks.

BREAKING PROJECTS INTO TASKS

In the end, all business relies on individual people making individual choices about their activities. Each person on your team needs to constantly ask and answer the question "What is the best use of my time right now?" A team whose members are focused will always outperform a team whose members are wasting time. Your team must make sure all assigned tasks are helping to achieve the larger goals.

Breaking projects into individual tasks helps the people on your team plan their time effectively. Tasks are individual activities that have been defined using the SMART model. At the end of a planning meeting, each person should walk away with a list of tasks and a timetable stating when goals are expected to be achieved.

When people start defining tasks, they are confronted by the question of detail. "How detailed should the tasks be?" For example, consider the task of delivering a newsletter. You could define this with different levels of detail:

- Carl will gather information for a newsletter by May 1.
- Carl will format the newsletter by May 7.
- Carl will make copies of the newsletter by May 14.
- Carl will distribute the newsletter in mailboxes by May 15.

Or you could just say:

- Carl will create and distribute a newsletter to the team by May 15.

There is no level of detail that works best in all cases. Your team and the individual responsible for owning the task need to decide the level of detail needed at the time the tasks are defined. Here are some things to consider when making that decision:

- **Experience.** How experienced is the person doing the task? If Carl has created many newsletters in his career, then the simple one-line task should be sufficient. If Carl has no experience with planning a newsletter, a detailed approach will be more helpful.
- **Criticality of the task.** Is this task critical to the team's success? If so, then you and the team will want to monitor it carefully and

RECOGNIZE GENIUS II: MAKING IT LOOK SIMPLE

Chess is a complicated game. It starts out with the same board, but after only three moves there are dozens of things to worry about; after ten moves it's easy to be overwhelmed. We think, "Do I move the knight, or do I take his pawn? When do I take out my queen? I saw *Searching for Bobby Fischer*. What did they say? Maybe I should just castle. . . ." The complexity is overwhelming.

Unless you're good at chess. The chess master would think there are only two moves worth considering; the rest of them are obviously inferior. The master would look at the board and say, "Develop the pieces, move your bishop to a central square, and then castle." The right move is obvious after you talk to the master.

Geniuses make things simple because they are able to draw a mental map of the situation, regardless of the field of study. They can "see" relationships between people, markets, products, or political alliances. When you ask them a question, they can read from their mental map and give you a simple solution. Mozart didn't say that he wrote music; he said that he "copied it out." He could write music while drinking beer, playing pool, or having a conversation, because all he was doing was copying the music from his head onto paper. Stephen King has likened writing a story to uncovering a fossil; the story is already there—he is just discovering it.

You can recognize genius by the simplicity of a genius's answers to the questions of what and why. The genius will tell you what to do in simple terms: "Move your bishop to a central square." If you ask why, the genius will also answer simply: "Because you can't do anything until you get your pieces off their home squares." Geniuses are very clear.

When you hire, expect to hire geniuses. Find people who can tell you what they would do in a complex situation and why they would do it. Look for confidence and a sense that they are simply reading the answer off a mental map. If they look like they are figuring it out as they go along, they are unlikely to be geniuses.

perhaps create more interim deadlines and tasks. You have to watch critical areas carefully.

→ **Ability to catch up.** Can the owner catch up if there is a delay? If Carl doesn't have any material by May 11, there is little chance the newsletter will make the May 15 deadline. Thus continuous updates are the best approach.

At the end of this process, the team will have a list of tasks. Each task will have a single owner and a date. Your team members now know where to focus their time. Team members who are doing tasks that are not on the task sheet can also see either that they are not helping the team achieve its goals or that the planning process missed something important. Both pieces of information are valuable.

Example of the Planning Process

Here is an example of the planning process for a team that has committed itself to achieving the result of being rated as "good" or "great" by 90 percent of its customers by the end of the following quarter. The team will need to create several projects to implement this result:

1. **Design a measuring system.** If the company doesn't have a way of measuring customer response, someone on the team needs to take ownership of creating a customer-response tracking system.
2. **Measure current status.** Once the measuring system is in place, the team needs to measure how customers currently rate the team's performance.
3. **Discover the root cause of the current status.** If the team is currently not achieving its goal of being rated "good" or "great" by 90 percent of customers, the underlying reasons for this need to be determined.

These projects may involve the whole team or only certain members. The team needs to assign owners and create SMART objectives for these projects. A SMART definition for this project would look like the following:

Design a measuring system: Present the results of a sample customer-service survey to the team by May 31.

Notice that the design of the measuring system is measured by its ability to deliver some data to the group. This follows the SMART model for describing a goal:

+ **Specific.** The owners of the project must provide specific results. The team can clearly see when the sample survey is delivered.
+ **Measurable.** You can measure whether the project has been delivered by whether the sample report is ready.
+ **Achievable.** Those who sign up for the project must believe it can be accomplished.
+ **Relevant.** We must have a customer-survey system to deliver on a goal that measures customer satisfaction. So this project is relevant to the overall goal.
+ **Time-bounded.** The team must meet a deadline of May 31.

The project as it's currently defined is still very high level. You could not put "Create a customer survey system and deliver a test poll" on your daily or weekly task list. We will break this project down into tasks to make it more measurable:

+ Marie will meet with the IT department to see if they have recommendations for a customer-response tracking system. She will report IT's recommendations to the team next week.
+ Manoj will deliver a report that describes companies who will do a customer survey for us to our team meeting next week.

Once your team has created the plan, you may want to outline it in single-page format so that everyone on your team understands what must be done. One way to do this is with a spreadsheet. Figure 10.2 is an example of a single-sheet format. This plan will become the basis for the feedback part of your team's operating system.

Keeping Track of Progress

It's essential that your team have a feedback mechanism for tracking tasks. This can be done in a variety of ways.

- You can have individuals e-mail the team when they complete a task.
- You can check personally on tasks and mark them off.
- You can set up a team Web log where people submit their progress reports.
- You can use a microblogging service to let team members submit short statuses as they complete tasks.

As people report completed tasks, have someone check off the tasks and report the status back to the team. This person needs to alert the team if task completion is running late. Make sure your tracker has a talent for highly disciplined tasks. The person doesn't necessarily have to have a leadership position. You just need someone

FIGURE 10.2

A PLANNING EXAMPLE

TEAM GOAL
90% of our customers rate us as good or great by the end of the year

PROJECT
Owner: Julia
Measure current satisfaction by April 15th

Task	Owner	Date
Deliver a report of current internal survey capabilities	Marie	Feb. 15
Deliver a report of commercial measurement services	Manoj	Feb. 15
Decide on whether to use commercial service or internal system	Team	Feb. 22
Determine the sample size needed to make a meaningful measurement	Andrea	March 01
Implement a survey using chosen services	Harry	March 15
Deliver a current measurement of customer satisfaction	Harry	April 15

who is adept at keeping track of details. If you enjoy details, then this is a good job for you. If you don't enjoy details, pick someone on your team to do it.

Each week, team members need a report on how they are doing relative to their tasks. If someone is not meeting deadlines, team members should be willing to step forward and help that person or team get back on track. This is true collaboration.

A clearly defined plan of action like this one is the cornerstone of great team execution. A plan makes it clear for everyone to see what the team needs to accomplish and when people are doing tasks that support the team's goals. Once you've got a plan like this in place, you are ready to move to the day-to-day execution process that keeps you on track.

Creating a plan is an exciting part of the recovery process. In this part, you took a group of people who have just been through a traumatic experience and helped them create goals, roles, and a plan to deliver to the company.

EXECUTING YOUR PLAN

N ow it's time to connect your people to the team's mission and goals through a team plan and individual plans that tie your team members' motivations to their jobs. This is where many people think management starts, but they have a hard time of it because they haven't built a collaborative team, given them a clear challenge, or chosen the right people for the jobs.

Now that you've done all those things, these tasks should be relatively easy. It's just a matter of executing over the three weeks.

CONNECT

DELIVERABLE	DESCRIPTION	DATE
Hold three feed-back sessions.	Create a tradition of execution by getting constant feedback about the tasks and helping the team devise new plans to achieve the goals (see Chapter 11).	Weeks 10, 11, 12
Create win-win agreements.	Help team members find their internal motivation for fulfilling their roles and make an explicit agreement with each person to help the person achieve personal goals from work (see Chapter 12).	Week 11

At this point, we've got a team of people with a mission and a specific set of SMART goals. We're now ready to answer two questions to connect our people to the goals:

✦ How do we achieve these goals?
✦ Why do we achieve these goals?

The first question—how?—deals with our plan for achieving our goals. We need to create a plan that connects the people on our team to specific tasks that will accomplish the goals. We will create that plan within the context of an operating system that keeps our team on task. Execution breeds confidence, and we'll see how to create a system to focus our team, achieve our goals, and celebrate our wins.

How is only one half of the equation when it comes to achieving our team's goals. We also need to understand why. More specifically, we need to understand why each person on the team should be invested in achieving the team's goals. What is in it for them personally that makes this job a means to achieve what they want in life? Connecting people to the goals is the key to unstoppable motivation.

We'll cover two topics in discussing the task of connecting:

➤ The beauty of execution
➤ Cultivating unstoppable motivation

Once you have this skill under your belt, you'll have a team of highly motivated people working in concert.

11

THE BEAUTY OF
EXECUTION

SUCCESSFUL UPPER-LEVEL MANAGERS run the gamut of personality types. Some are flamboyant, and some are reserved. Some are great intellects, while others are incredible speakers. In fact, if you look for a common trait among upper management, you will find only one—successful managers get things done. They execute.

Now, some managers leave a wake of bodies wherever they go. These managers give execution a bad name. They evoke an image of the hard-driving, intimidating boss who yells at people, pounds the table, and fires the unlucky. I once had a manager who had one question when he saw that one of his departments hadn't reached its goal: "Who will be fired because of this?"

You do not want to be this kind of manager. These kinds of managers may get short-term results, but this comes at the expense of their long-term career and the future well-being of the company. These managers may be hired to do a dirty job, but they'll never be asked to run a successful company.

On the other hand, some managers don't demand enough execution. They feel that collaborative leadership means they cannot demand execution from their team or themselves. They, too, are missing the point. Being a collaborative leader does not mean you need to accept anything less than excellent execution from yourself or your team. It does mean you build a team of people who expect excellence from each other. In this chapter, you'll learn how to manage the balance between execution and collaborative leadership.

EXECUTION IS NONNEGOTIABLE

Upper-level managers have a simple view of you and your team. If you do what you tell them you are going to do, you are successful and will be rewarded. If you don't, you are just another problem they need to deal with. Execution is black and white. Either you are reliable or you aren't. If you aren't, then other people spend time and energy making backup plans to cover your failure to deliver. Your goal is to be a pillar of strength, not a point of weakness.

I observed one person in a company who had a powerful habit. He would use the word "Done" to signify that he had taken on a task. Meetings would go like this:

Bill's manager: "Bill, I need you to call Axeworth Associates and set up a joint seminar."

Bill: "Done."

In one word, Bill had said that he had accepted the assignment, and because he had accepted the assignment, it could already be considered completed. That is incredible confidence and execution skill. As a member of Bill's team, you didn't worry about any task Bill accepted. You knew that if Bill was on it, the task was in good hands.

Bill went on to start his own company and became a millionaire because he kept his commitments and executed results.

Does your group match this level of execution? More important, do you? This is a key question to your group's success and your own. There is nothing more energizing to a team than to set challenging goals for itself and reach them. There is nothing more depressing than to see goal after goal drop by the wayside, unmet.

There are people who are so burned out on unmet goals that they are unwilling to set new ones. You may have such individuals in your group, particularly after a layoff. Rather than saying they will accomplish something, they say they will try. Watch out for the word *try* in a meeting. If people tell you they will "try" to accomplish something, they are telling you right up front that they will not accomplish it. As Yoda said in *Return of the Jedi*: "Do or do not. There is no 'try.'"

Driving execution in a team may seem like the opposite of what we've been talking about up until this point. Most of this book has focused on collaborative leadership, shared power, and joint commitments. Suddenly we're talking about hard-nosed execution. Isn't that inconsistent? No.

Soft Leadership and Hard Management

We've discussed many concepts in this book that people would consider "soft management." The collaborative style of management pushes responsibility for results down to the team. It seeks to find jobs where people can succeed. Collaborative management employs Quaker meetings and takes people's feelings into account.

Many people confuse this kind of soft leadership with soft execution. When they hear that a manager worries about missions, feelings, and roles, they picture a team that is soft on hard work and results. Nothing could be further from the truth.

Many people confuse collaborative management with weak management. There is an enormous difference. Weak managers assign goals to their employees and then let the employees off the hook if the goals are not achieved. Collaborative managers work with employees to set goals that are achievable and meet the company's needs. They then create an environment that measures results and expects the team and its members to meet commitments.

In the end, the weak managers create depressed and unmotivated teams. People on the team are never able to test themselves or improve because they have no power to set goals and no driving need to meet them. Execution-focused managers create excited teams who have tested themselves against the world and prevailed.

Great managers expect to win, and they build teams of people who expect to win. Winning is a mind-set and a process. Winning teams know they can't control everything that will happen to them. But once they understand a situation, they figure out what they need to do to recover from the setback, and then they go out and try to make it happen. If one plan doesn't work, they regroup and try another approach.

Even in defeat, great teams will feel a sense of accomplishment because they know they did their absolute best to achieve the goal. When you create a great team, you also create an environment where people know they have spent themselves on a worthy cause. This is the benefit of execution-oriented management.

FIRE PEOPLE FAST

Given that you've just gone through a layoff, it may seem odd to think about firing people. It's not as unusual as you might think. Justice isn't always done in a layoff, and you may have been handed a new group to run. Inside that group you may find someone who is just not going to work out.

Now, I'm not saying that you should *decide* to fire people quickly. There may be a lot going on, especially after a layoff, that explains problem employee behavior, and there are steps to follow in that instance. I'm saying that once *you decide* to fire someone you should do it immediately if possible and very soon if not.

Firing people is stressful. It will consume your mind as you think about

the best way to break the news, when to break the news, how to break the news. If you're wasting time fretting over a firing, you are shortchanging the rest of your team.

Delaying the firing is also not fair to the team member. If you're looking at the person and thinking, "Dead man walking," you're not serving him. You're just serving yourself, because you are trying to put off a difficult conversation. Remember, too, that every day he's sitting in a dead job he's missing opportunities to get a new job. You're not doing him any favors by keeping him around.

Bills, cavities, and firings are three things that don't get better with time. Fire quickly and move on.

THE BOYD LOOP: ENGINE OF EXECUTION

In the 1970s John Boyd, a captain in the U.S. Air Force, analyzed air combat in the Korean War. This combat was exceptionally successful: U.S. pilots had a ten-to-one kill ratio. This was especially interesting to the air force because the U.S. fighter plane, the F-86, was supposedly inferior to its Korean counterpart, the MiG-15, in almost every way. The MiG-15 accelerated faster and turned more quickly than the F-86, yet the U.S. pilots still won more than 90 percent of their engagements.

It turned out that the F-86 did have two advantages over the MiG-15. First, the pilot in an F-86 had a better line of sight; and second, the hydraulic controls in the F-86 allowed the U.S. pilots to switch between maneuvers more quickly. Given these facts, John Boyd developed the concept of the Boyd Loop and used it to explain the ten-to-one disparity in results.

The Boyd Loop (see Figure 11.1) describes how an individual or a team responds to changing conditions. There are four stages to the cycle:

- **Observe.** This is data gathering, when you collect the raw data of where you are or your team is, relative to your goal.
- **Orient.** Once you gather the data, you need to interpret it. Are you positioned favorably or not? What are your options given the current situation?
- **Decide.** After you've identified several options, you need to decide which action to take to improve your position.
- **Act.** Take the action you (or your team) have decided on and execute it with speed and efficiency. Then go back to the beginning of the loop to see how you did.

Boyd found that U.S. pilots created tactics that took advantage of their superior ability to observe and respond. They devised maneuvers that forced a response from their opponent. They then switched to the next maneuver before the Korean pilots had time

FIGURE 11.1 **THE BOYD LOOP**

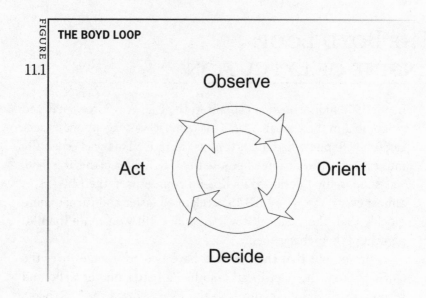

to adapt. Their opponent ended up caught a step behind and lost ground with every maneuver. Eventually their opponent was forced into a bad position and shot down.

Boyd generalized this approach to combat to other forms of competition. The Boyd Loop was eventually applied to business, where its application is obvious. Business history is littered with companies that could not respond quickly enough to competitive moves from faster rivals.

We've all been on teams that have not tried to execute a single Boyd Loop. These teams create a goal at the beginning of the year and create a plan to attack the goal. Then they simply go to work each day and look at the goal at the end of the year. If the goal has been met, great. If it's been missed, the team shrugs and establishes a new, perhaps lesser, goal for next year.

There are also managers who have no concept of the Boyd Loop. Remember the manager mentioned earlier who wanted to know who would be fired because a department had failed to complete a goal? He would assign a goal to his team at the beginning of the year and then wait to see who achieved it. Those who made their goals were rewarded; the others were punished and/or fired.

The Boyd Loop holds the key to great execution. Great managers help their team execute this loop as quickly and effectively as possible. They know that the plan a team formulates at the beginning of the year is rarely the plan that accomplishes the goal and that the team will need to modify the plan many times to take new information and changing conditions into account.

This is where accountability comes into the picture. All team members must be able to make a meaningful contribution to the Boyd Loop. While great managers don't punish people for missing arbitrary goals, they must be able to remove people who are not performing their part of the Boyd Loop. Here are some accountability requirements and problems, discussed in terms of the Boyd Loop.

Observe

Observation is measuring how you are doing against the current plan and making sure you are getting the results you expect. All team members must be able to apprise the team regarding the status of their projects and let the team know when things change.

This is the purpose of the feedback system created during the planning stage. Your team must show the discipline to constantly follow through on this system. If you and the team allow the system to slip, you will not be able to accurately observe your progress.

People can exhibit two problems in this part of the Boyd Loop. One is more serious than the other, but both could require you to remove a team member. The first is feedback neglect. In this situation, the person constantly forgets to engage in the feedback process. This can be seen as late status reports, lack of a clear description of the status of tasks, or simple refusal to participate.

You cannot let this situation fester. If someone on your team is neglecting to provide feedback, you need to point out the lapse and insist that he or she adhere to the feedback program. If you involve your team in the process, it will probably exert peer pressure on the offending team member long before you need to step in.

The second issue is hiding problems. This is a severe problem, and you will need to remove a team member who does this consistently. Hiding problems has two consequences. The first is that it compounds the problem. It is easy to fix problems if they are addressed at the initial stages. By hiding problems, a team member makes it more difficult to recover later on.

Another bad side to hiding problems is that it destroys the team's trust. This is a basic violation of the idea that the team is working together to meet the goals. Team members who hide problems obviously consider their own reputation more important than the team's goals.

Hiding problems is a serious breach. One man, Nick Leeson, completely destroyed the Barings Bank by hiding his mistakes. Leeson worked for Barings as an options trader. He made some bad trades and started to fall behind. Rather than let his superiors know about his mistakes, he hid his losses and continued to make larger and larger trades in an effort to recoup the money.

As he dug his hole deeper, Leeson became more desperate. Finally, he simply disappeared from his desk in an attempt to return to England before he was arrested on fraud charges. When his superiors finally caught on, they learned that Leeson had lost more than $1.3 billion. The bank was wiped out. Investors lost all their savings, and more than twelve hundred employees lost their jobs.

While it's unlikely that one employee could destroy your company, it is easy for a single employee to create a situation from which the team cannot recover. You must make it clear to everyone that people are not punished for problems. Instead, they are praised for bringing the team's attention to problems early on. Observation is the key to the Boyd Loop. You need to make sure your team knows where it is headed and has the information it needs to respond to changes.

Orient

In his book *Think Like a Grandmaster*, chess grandmaster Alexander Kotov reveals how great chess players analyze complicated positions. They choose several possible moves to consider.

USE AVAILABLE TECHNOLOGY

t's been said that in a bad economy there are only two kinds of people: overworked and laid off. Layoffs produce overworked people as the company tries to become more productive. Make sure you rise to the challenge and become more productive using modern technology.

Search tools are one of the best time-saving technologies available. These tools don't search the Web; instead, they search your computer. They index every file and every e-mail in an enormous database and allow you to find data by simply typing some words into a text box.

If you are one of those folks who spends an hour a day moving e-mails out of your in-box and into folders, you can stop doing it now because search tools have come to the rescue. Instead of wasting time moving e-mails into folders, leave them in the in-box. Let your search tool index them, and then you can find any e-mails you want by typing in a couple of key words.

If your IT department limits your in-box, archive your e-mails into an e-mail file on your computer and then tell the search tool where to find the new e-mails. The search tool will index the archived e-mail as well as your in-box, and you'll be able to find any e-mail.

Once you've found a system you like, share it with your team. They'll notice your productivity focus, and you will win converts to your new, more efficient way of life.

Then they analyze each of these candidate moves in turn as deeply as necessary.

Inexperienced chess players don't follow this process. They look at one move, analyze it a little, jump to another move and analyze that for a while, and then they jump to a third move. Often they go back to the first move and repeat the process. Sometimes, because of time constraints or exhaustion, they'll see a completely different fourth move and make it with no analysis at all. This choice almost always ends in disaster.

When a team orients itself, it needs to develop candidate moves before it can analyze any of them. For example, say you have a team of engineers that has just learned the chip it is relying on will be delivered six months late. The engineers need to come up with a plan that will deliver their project on time without the chip. They may develop several candidate moves:

- They can buy a similar chip from another vendor and modify the design.
- They can design their own chip.
- They can modify their software to take the lack of the chip into consideration.

They don't need to analyze these options at this point or argue about which is better. They simply need to make a list of several possible options.

Decide

Once the team has created several candidate moves, it needs to decide among them. This is the step at which team members need to value each other's differences and work together to come up with the best solution. If a team is working toward a common goal, this can be a rewarding process. If the team is mired in personal battles or has individual members who are trying to pad their own egos, this is a very difficult process.

This is where you need to watch your team in action and decide on the level of teamwork it can handle. If individual members cannot elevate their thinking to take the team's needs into account, you'll need to make decisions. However, you should not settle for this outcome. You should keep trying to push your team to make increasingly complicated decisions.

There are several enemies to the process you should notice and fix. If you see an employee engaged in one of these, you must either help that person become a better contributor to the Boyd Loop or remove the person from the decision process:

- **Ego.** People who become attached to their ideas and fight for them simply out of ego will slow a team down. Team members need to derive their satisfaction from the team's performance, not from the ego boost of having their idea implemented.

✦ **Unwillingness to share ideas.** All team members have an obligation to voice their concerns in an environment of exploration. People need to debate ideas and come to the best solution rather than try to make each other look good.

✦ **Disengagement and dissent.** Some people feel that meetings are a waste of time and are unwilling to help the team come to a decision. The disengagement problem becomes worse when the person turns into a Monday-morning quarterback and complains about the decision. This is poison to the process. Anyone who disengages from the process must be willing to accept the team's decision.

Your team needs everyone's participation if it is going to make good decisions. By pressing people to contribute to the decision process, you will ensure that you have gathered the best of everyone's thinking and that you have left the decision-making process with buy-in to the team's decision.

USE CALENDAR SOFTWARE TO KEEP PROJECTS ON TRACK

Tracking projects to completion is an important skill when managing after a layoff. Your company needs all its employees to work smarter, create more with less, and keep a close eye on deliverables.

One way to keep track of a project is to use your calendar software as a simple project tracker. You do this by adding project deadlines to your team's calendars as fifteen-minute meetings, such as "E-mail completed reports to me."

The beauty of this system is that it works regardless of the task-tracking mechanism your team members choose. While people may have different task-tracking tools, they all use the same calendaring software, and usually you can add appointments to other people's calendars the same way that you invite them to meetings.

Another advantage is that people will notice the deadlines. People check their calendars religiously, even if they are not as religious about checking their task-tracking tool. People will see that deadline approaching and will eventually get a pop-up reminding them of the impending event.

Act

Once the team has made a decision, it is time to act. The team must create new objectives and tasks that match the new plan, and these must go into the feedback system. It's now time to execute aggressively to make the new plan come to life. Remember the phrase "A good plan executed violently today is better than a perfect plan executed tomorrow." This attitude is essential for a fast Boyd Loop. You need to try new things so you can get feedback quickly and modify your approach.

The biggest performance problem you'll see is people who do not act—specifically, people who let task after task slip by them without getting their work done. If the team has created a reasonable plan and one person is not meeting the goals, that person is a problem employee.

You will have to move sooner rather than later in these cases. You'll need to use the job-description matrix to determine whether

---

LEAVE THE MEETING WITH A NEXT STEP

It happens every day in conference rooms across the world. People sit together and discuss a problem. Then they reach the end of the conversation. There is nothing more to say, but the hour isn't up yet, so nobody wants to end the meeting. There is an awkward silence; then somebody starts gathering papers. Finally everybody leaves, and in doing so they commit a cardinal sin against execution. They haven't explicitly named the next step.

Every meeting should end with a clearly defined next step. Presumably, you met to discuss some problem. Presumably, you want the problem solved. Presumably, there are things you need to do to solve the problem. Since there are things you need to do to solve the problem, there must be one thing that you need to do first.

Name that first thing. Give it a date and an owner and a specific, measurable result. Walk away from that meeting with a promise of the next step.

If you can't find a next step, you and your team haven't fully understood the problem. Determine what you need to figure out the first step. Do you need information? Find it. Do you need buy-in? Set up a meeting with the stakeholders. Do you need to do something else before you can complete the first step? Make that the first step.

If every meeting results in a first step, every meeting will be valuable. So make sure you and your team name that first step.

this person lacks the basic talent or training to complete the tasks. If talent and training are not an issue, you may have a problem with motivation or prioritization.

This is a case in which it is OK to remove someone from a team who is not meeting deadlines. If the person is consistently missing reasonable deadlines and is not taking, or cannot take, the steps necessary to fix the problem, it is time to find a new team member. The person is either not suited for or not interested in the job. In either case, good teams will demand this person's dismissal.

The Boyd Loop is the engine of your execution machine. You do not create an execution machine by firing people who miss deadlines. You create an execution machine by teaching your team members to execute the Boyd Loop and by requiring that everyone on the team take an active role in delivering results.

Execution Starts with You

There is a joke about a great hunting dog named "Salesperson" who would run around and flush out birds until he was renamed "Sales Manager"; then he would just sit on his tail and bark. The cliché of a great individual contributor being turned into a poor manager often leads people to speculate about why companies put their best individual contributors in a management position when that is clearly not their strong suit. Is upper-level management blind to what happens? Of course not.

Companies promote the best individual contributors to management because they see the drive and initiative of these individuals and hope that these qualities will be transferred to a team of people. In short, they see an individual who exhibits great execution, and they put that person in a position to influence others to achieve the same level of execution.

Execution starts with you. Your team members will watch you to set their own levels of motivation and drive. They know the speed of the leader is the speed of the pack. If you want your team to exhibit exceptional execution, you need to lead the way. Here are some places where you can demonstrate your commitment to execution:

- **Make commitments.** Some people try to avoid being measured on how well they execute tasks and goals by avoiding commitments. Don't be one of these! Set dates for when you'll complete tasks and then complete the tasks. If you can't complete the task because of some emergency, proactively contact the stakeholders, explain the problem, and set a new date.
- **Be early.** This is a simple rule, but hardly anyone takes it seriously. If a meeting starts at 9:00 A.M., be in your chair at 8:58 A.M. Remember, there is no such thing as "on time." You are either early or late. Be early.
- **Return voice mails and e-mails.** Develop a reputation for always getting back to people. One extremely successful manager I met (who ran for governor of Massachusetts in addition to running his business) had a simple rule for voice mail messages. He returned them all. He even returned voice mails to solicitors and people he didn't know. If you called him and left a message, he would call you back—even if just to leave you a message. This behavior builds discipline and execution. Your team will notice it and emulate you.

By taking a personal stand for execution in the way you conduct yourself and conduct business, you will show your team what it takes to succeed.

CREATING A FEEDBACK PROCESS

Now it's time to link the Boyd Loop back to your planning process. The planning process we discussed uses goals, projects, and tasks to make a plan. We will add the feedback process into this system to capture the full power of the Boyd Loop.

A feedback process is simply a way of checking that tasks are being done on time (observing) so you can make new plans if necessary (orienting). There are many ways to create feedback processes. You can use any of them as long as they give the team a clear picture of what is going on. Here are a few approaches.

Feedback by Wandering About

In this system, you gather feedback from your team by visiting each person individually and gathering his or her status on each task. This approach gives you a clear picture of status and an opportunity to help people who are having trouble meeting their goals.

The disadvantage here is that you are the only person with the whole picture. This makes teamwork difficult. If you use this system, you should send the team a weekly status report. Some managers will delegate feedback gathering to a person in the group. This person will go around the group and record how people are doing against their tasks and deliver a report to the team. This may be an advantage if you are not available weekly or if you prefer to let someone else focus on the detailed work of task management.

Status Reports

In this system you send an e-mail requesting status from all your team members, and they send you back their status. Then you combine the responses into a status report that you can send up to your manager and down to the team.

This is an efficient system, but it robs you of the chance to coach people at the time they present their status. Also, people tend to be less frank about their situation when they have to write it down, so you may get skewed status updates.

Status E-Mails

This is a lightweight status system. In this system your folks send a two-sentence e-mail to the team every time they complete a task.

You have the master list of tasks, so you check off that task and distribute the list back to the team with your observations. This is a very inexpensive system and works well with geographically dispersed teams.

The feedback system you choose is not as important as the fact that you choose one. You must create a culture of feedback, accountability, and execution in your team. A feedback system is the linchpin of this approach to execution. Whichever system you and your team choose, you must be faithful about following it and keeping track of deliverables. It's the only way your team will get the information it needs to execute the Boyd Loop.

ORGANIZE YOUR NEXT PROJECT

In his landmark productivity book *Getting Things Done*, David Allen recommends five steps that he associates with planning any project. I use these steps myself, so I'm sharing them here.

All projects, which are defined as tasks that take more than one step to resolve, have five natural steps to planning:

1. **Defining the purpose and principles.** Why are we doing this?
2. **Envisioning the outcome.** What does success look like?
3. **Brainstorming.** What are all the things we need to do to accomplish this goal?
4. **Organizing.** What is the best order in which to do the steps?
5. **Identifying next actions.** What are the very next steps we need to take?

We deliver our projects quickly and effectively when we follow these steps.

The opposite is to not plan the project at all. This usually leads us to follow the steps in the reverse order. For example, let's say we want to organize a sales trip.

We don't know what to do next, so we think we need to get organized. This causes us to start to brainstorm everything we have to do, and that gets us to picture what we're trying to accomplish. Finally we reach the point where we ask "Why?"

We want to go on the sales trip to create leads for the product. We're going to travel by car to save money. We picture driving down the East Coast visiting customers as we go, so that no trip between customers is too long. Then we brainstorm a list of customers and organize the list by state. Finally, we get to the next step: call potential customers and set up visits.

Use these five steps to organize your next project. You'll be amazed at how quickly it comes together.

USE A PRIORITIZATION GRID

Prioritization is a fact of business life. We cannot do everything that is asked of us; we must make choices.

We can make these choices individually or as teams, but in both cases we need to have a standard way of prioritizing multiple items. A prioritization grid fits the bill.

A prioritization grid gives us a systematic way to prioritize multiple tasks, options, goals, or even people. Here's an example of using a prioritization graph.

Let's say that we want to pick dessert for the upcoming Fun Friday company get-together. We have a team of people who have nominated several desserts: ice cream, pie, pudding, cookies. We would prioritize these options by drawing a grid similar to the one shown here:

	A Ice Cream	B Pie	C Pudding	D Cookies
A Ice Cream		B	A	A
B Pie			B	B
C Pudding				D

The table allowed us, as a team, to compare each of the options. Did we want ice cream more than pie? No. So pie won, and we placed a *B* in that grid location. Did we want ice cream more than pudding? Yes. So we put an *A* in that grid location. We work our way down through the options, making comparisons between two items. Then we count the letters, as shown here.

Option	Votes
Pie	3
Ice Cream	2
Cookies	1
Pudding	0

It looks like we're going with pie.

We can use prioritization grids in many ways. We can either count all the letters, or we can record a weight next to each comparison where *1* means hardly any difference and *3* means there is an obvious difference.

This tool will keep your team focused and on track.

MANAGE FOR EXECUTION

You start by demonstrating execution to your team. Then you manage your team to promote and create an execution culture. Here are some things you can do to promote execution.

➤ **Talk about execution.** Discuss successful examples of execution that you see in your team and in other teams. Use them as case studies in department and one-on-one meetings with your employees, peer group, and manager.

➤ **Praise execution.** When one of your team members executes a task or project effectively, commend the person. Let people see what you value and what you think is important.

➤ **Expect recovery plans.** Execution means taking responsibility for commitments and doing what it takes to deliver. When people bring a problem to you, give it back to them until they come back with possible solutions and a recovery plan.

➤ **Give prompt feedback.** If someone on your team is interfering with execution, act swiftly. Address the behavior and how you believe it interferes with the Boyd Loop.

Execution is the basic building block of business success and careers. Your career will skyrocket (as will your personal sense of job security) when you develop a reputation as someone who delivers on promises. As a manager you are dependent on your team to deliver your results. By focusing on the Boyd Loop and making sure your team members participate in the process and respect it, you will create a team that delivers on its promises.

12

CULTIVATING
UNSTOPPABLE
MOTIVATION

LAYOFFS ARE A way of life in our economy. Companies lay people off almost as frequently in good times as in bad. The highly flexible and unforgiving global economy makes it impossible for companies to create an environment of long-term job security for its people and still be competitive.

Given this, how can you get people to commit to a company that can't commit to them? People once traded commitment for job security. Today that deal is dead. You need to make a new deal that doesn't include job security and still encourages commitment from the employees. It's a solvable problem, but you'll need to think differently.

Albert Einstein said, "The significant problems we have cannot be solved at the same level of thinking with which we created them." To solve the commitment problem, we need to look at the current way of thinking and move beyond it.

Many people still look for a way to find job security. Most employees make implicit deals with their company in which they trade commitment for job security. However, changes in the business environment have made this an impossible deal.

Unfortunately, most employees haven't fully accepted this change. Though they agree that there is no job security, they respond to this situation by complaining about how difficult it is to find a secure job. They are missing the point.

People can solve this problem only by thinking at a new level. They need to embrace the situation and stop looking for something that doesn't exist. They need to stop thinking about themselves as employees and start thinking about themselves as independent contractors.

People who think of themselves as independent contractors think of their employers as their customers. True, they may have only one customer, and it may make up 100 percent of their income, but they still view the company as a customer—not as a surrogate parent. Truly independent people realize that their name is written on a pink slip the day they join a company; it's just waiting for a delivery date. Rather than being depressed by this knowledge, independent people acknowledge that as a fact. They also know they would leave the company if a better opportunity presented itself.

Once employees think of themselves as independent contractors, they will engage in behaviors that protect them from layoffs. They will build up a financial nest egg to carry them between jobs. They will join networking groups in their industry so they can quickly start a word-of-mouth job search. They will have their résumé in circulation even when they are not looking. Some managers would be threatened by these actions. You should embrace them as the signs that your team is mature and independent and will recover quickly from the next layoff.

As a manager, you need to encourage your employees to think of themselves as independent. This may be a radical approach in some organizations. Many managers discourage independence. They subtly threaten employees about considering other options. They speak highly of "loyal" employees who have been with the company for a long time. They may feel personally threatened to hear that an employee is looking at other options.

In the short term, that makes sense. Turnover is expensive. Managers are trained to maintain a high retention rate. But managers who discourage independence are selling out their employees. This is the wrong approach for two reasons:

- It is unethical to encourage dependence in somebody if you cannot offer that person security. This is like asking someone to become dependent on your water supply when you know the reservoir is almost empty.
- Since you cannot provide job security, you have nothing to offer dependent employees. If you can't offer anything to dependent employees, why create them? Instead, create employees who value what you can offer.

Great managers encourage independence. They know that there is no job security and that the people on their teams will move on to new adventures. They encourage learning and help their employees improve their skills. They'll hire people who can do the job, even if those people have had many other jobs. When the inevitable layoffs come, these managers have a great way to get commitment from the remaining employees—training.

Great managers help employees embrace the fact that they will have other jobs in their lives. They offer their employees interesting work that will build skills. Great managers tell employees, "I cannot guarantee that we'll have jobs here in the future. But I can guarantee that if you work for me you'll have experiences that improve your skills so you can get a new job quickly."

To create a "layoff-proof" team, you need to change the kind of commitment you offer people. Rather than offer them job security or a bright future with the company, offer them a chance to improve their skills and to make money doing something they enjoy.

Employees who are motivated by the work and the ability to improve their skills are immune to the lack of job security. They love what they do, and they appreciate the chance to improve, so they'll happily stay as long as the company will have them. They will also assume responsibility for their long-term financial well-being and maintain their networking relationships. When the next layoff happens, your team will have the skills and the mind-set to bounce back quickly. They are layoff-proof.

The new economy, and the need to create layoff-proof employees, gives you the key to motivating employees in a twenty-first-century economy. Excellent employees will keep themselves mobile and able to switch jobs quickly. That freedom leads to a new model of motivation.

IMPLEMENT TO-DO LIST SYSTEMS

Choose and implement a to-do list system. The days are over when you and your team could keep action items in your heads. Get a to-do list system and use it.

There are two parts to a to-do list system. One is the methodology you use for tracking actions. Your methodology answers questions such as: "Do you prioritize your tasks?" "Do you have multiple lists?" "When do you check your lists?" "How do you check your lists?" Companies such as Franklin Covey and The David Allen Company deliver methodologies such as these.

Once you have your methodology, implement it. You can use systems as simple as paper or as complex as a Web-based to-do system that can be accessed from your browser or phone and allows you to send voice messages that are translated into text tasks. Again, choose the one that is most comfortable for you. The best to-do system is the one you will use.

You should evangelize your system to your team. Show them how well you can track tasks and how your system keeps you on top of your obligations. Show them how you can use the system to track their obligations for you. Make a big deal about it, and some of your folks will start doing it themselves.

To-do systems are like diets. Nobody wants to be told what kind of diet they should eat to lose weight. But when they see someone who used a particular plan successfully, they tend to ask about the diet and try it themselves.

Do not try to mandate a common system for your team. Oh, it sounds nice and efficient, but people hate the imposition. It is the fastest way to get yourself labeled as a micromanager. Instead, do three things: teach your team about task management, evangelize your approach, and hold them accountable for their tasks. If they know that you're tracking what they owe you, they will be sure to track it themselves.

CREATING REAL MOTIVATION

Some managers use the old Skinner models of motivation—when the monkey pushes the button, he gets a pellet. Of course, since few employees work for pellets, the managers need to create elaborate systems of rewards and punishments to get the job done.

In his classic *Harvard Business Review* article "One More Time: How Do You Motivate Employees?" Frederick Herzberg called these KITA (Kick in the Ass) management systems. They rely on managers combining kicks in the ass with rewards to get results, and they don't really motivate employees. If employees are engaging in actions simply to avoid punishment or to win rewards, they will stop working when the rewards disappear. This is especially distressing during layoff times, because there are usually few rewards available. Of course, the recent application of a KOTD (Kick Out the Door) to some employees can provoke temporary activity in the remaining employees.

The employees of companies who use KITA systems are not motivated; their managers are motivated. That is why the managers created the KITA system. In this situation the employees will do what it takes to manipulate the system and achieve their bonuses or keep their jobs for the minimum energy required.

Real motivation comes from within. People work hard, strive for achievement, and celebrate successes for their own reasons. It is common to see people put far more energy into their hobbies than into their jobs. Golf is an example of this and gives us clues to intrinsic motivation.

Why does anyone play golf? It's expensive, time-consuming, and frustrating, and there is little or no chance that any of us will become as great a golfer as Tiger Woods. People who have trouble getting to work at 9:00 A.M. will get up at 5:30 A.M. to play golf. This is the kind of motivation you want your employees to have on the job.

Let's use the example of golf to test the idea of KITA management. KITA management states that people will be motivated if you reward them for the right behavior and punish them for the wrong behavior. We can test our idea by seeing if our common KITA approaches are available to golfers.

- **Bonuses.** Do most golfers receive tremendous bonuses that motivate them to play? No. There are few professional golfers. In fact, golf is a very expensive hobby. So money is not the motivator.
- **Punishments.** Does someone punish golfers if they don't play golf or play it well? No. There are no external punishments that motivate golfers.
- **Career advancement.** Can you get a promotion within the golfing system? No. All golfers are at the same pay grade (usually $0). Some people may use golf as a social event to improve their careers at work, but these occasional events do not motivate most golfers.
- **High salaries, benefits, company cars, and expense accounts.** Golfers don't get any of these. They are not the reason golfers get up at 5:30 A.M.

So golfers are not responding to KITA motivation methods. Yet golfers demonstrate the motivation levels most managers would love to see. The motivation comes from somewhere else.

People play golf because they love the game and they enjoy the challenge of improving their skills. This is the kind of motivation you want from your team. You want people who love to do the job and enjoy the challenge of improving their skills.

If you've put people into roles that match their talents, you are likely to have people who love the job. These people will work hard for the intrinsic enjoyment of improvement. You have solved more than half of the motivation problem when you put the right people in the right roles.

Once you have the right people in the right roles, you must create an environment that encourages high performance. High-performance teams need systems that support their growth. Again, golf provides a great example of these kinds of systems.

Golf provides high-performing people with systems that support their efforts. These systems help people measure their success and show them where they need to improve. The following are systems that exist in golf that you can re-create in the workplace.

- **Clearly measured results.** Golf has a score that measures how well a golfer did that day. When you ask golfers how their day went, they tell you what they shot. They are measured clearly. Do your employees have a way to clearly measure their results?
- **Opportunity for growth.** Golfers constantly strive to improve themselves. In fact, when golfers compete, they often use a handicap system that measures how well they did relative to their average level of play. Do your employees have the opportunity to improve their skills?
- **Clear achievement.** Golfers have specific milestones that measure their progress and achievement. Their first sub-100 game and getting a birdie are clear achievements. What clear achievement levels exist for your people?
- **Opportunities for recognition.** While it's fun to hit the perfect shot, it's much more fun when you do it in front of other golfers. Golfers continually praise each other's successes, even when they are playing against one another. Do your employees get recognized by you, or the team, when they succeed?
- **Competition.** Golfers can compare themselves to others in a competitive environment. This is especially applicable to business when people play in teams. You don't want your employees to compete against each other. You want them to compete against other companies in the marketplace. Have you fostered a sense of healthy competition against rival companies?

From this list you can see that employees are motivated by fun jobs that give them an opportunity to grow and test themselves. Employees will motivate themselves when you create a clear way to measure progress and get recognition for success. This allows you to spend your time on coaching, planning, and other high-value activities.

If you've hired properly and put people into roles that use their talents, most of your people will consider their jobs fun. They will want to improve their strengths, and they'll see an opportunity for achievement. Since they are good at what they do, they'll have opportunities for recognition. Your next step is to create a plan with clearly defined milestones so they can measure their progress and keep score.

Meanwhile, though, what do you do about clear lack of motivation on the part of individual team members?

Addressing Low Motivation

When you have a problem employee who has the talent and skills to do the job, but who isn't doing the activity necessary to succeed, you are dealing with a problem of low motivation. There is one root cause for all motivation issues:

Low motivation comes from low priority. The problem employee is prioritizing something in life above work.

This is not to say that we require employees to make the job their top motivation in life. That kind of imbalance is unhealthy for them and ultimately for the company. Rather, the insight says that the employee has moved work so far down the priority chain that he is not accomplishing the tasks we need him to accomplish.

Motivation problems are often indicators of bigger problems in an employee's life. If the employee has a personal health concern, that is absolutely going to become a higher personal priority. The health concern could also be affecting someone in the employee's family. The health concern could also include substance abuse problems or psychological issues. All these issues will take a higher priority in a person's life.

Motivation problems could come from financial sources as well. Perhaps the employee has picked up a second job or has started a home-based business. Both of these are time-consuming activities and could be affecting priority.

INSTITUTE A NO E-MAIL/TEXT MESSAGE RULE

There are very few times that I lay down the law as a manager. I'm generally an easygoing guy, and I like my team members to take ownership of their deliverables, including the way they deliver them.

I'm no dictator, except when it comes to the question of sending e-mail or text messages in a training class. I think every manager deserves to lay down the law on at least one topic. Call it a pet peeve or an idiosyncrasy, but I will simply not stand for people on my team sending e-mails or text messages from their phones or laptops during a training class. I have three reasons for this:

+ **It's just plain rude.** I've taught training classes, and it's a lot of work. As an instructor you gather energy from seeing people looking at you and nodding. If, instead, you see people looking down at their phones, openly ignoring what you have to say, you get depressed and demoralized and give a much worse class.
+ **It's a waste of money.** The time for training classes costs at least $50 per hour per student.

The class has additional costs of paying the instructor, printing the materials, renting the room, and flying people in for the training. After spending all this money, I have no interest in watching someone on my team try to answer e-mail or texts.

+ **It's shortsighted.** Sharpening the saw, as Covey would say, is one of the most high-value activities available. We train our people because we believe that the time spent today on training will be paid back in time saved in the future. Unless, of course, the trainee is wasting this expensive and precious time by doing work that could be done at the desk on a normal day.

It's difficult today to ask our companies to invest in training our people. If we are blessed with upper managers who are farsighted enough to invest in training, we can't afford to let that investment go to waste.

And that's why I have, and recommend, a strict no e-mail/text message policy during training classes.

In the least dire case, the person may be more interested in her softball team, friends on the beach, or wedding-planning projects. The sources of low motivation come from every angle.

Handle all motivation problems the same way:

+ **Create an action plan of tangible results with the employee.** These are measurable results you need to see from the employee if the employee is going to keep the job. If the employee is going through a crisis, you might make this list very short and plan to backfill the employee's productivity.

- ➔ **Help the employee.** You are not a psychologist! You are not trained to help people through a family crisis. You are not a doctor. Be very clear on what you are not when it comes to helping an employee with issues. That said, your company may have an employee assistance program, and you may be able to backfill the workload for a while. Point the employee to the employee assistance program if you have one.

If the employee is working through motivation issues that don't require employee assistance, then help through coaching. Keep track of the activity levels, watch the tangible result carefully, and make sure the employee stays on track. Sometimes this is all you need to reconnect someone to the job.

Thinking Win-Win

You've now got a team with a plan. You also have team members with internal motivation to implement the plan. However, they may not explicitly see how working on the plan helps them achieve their personal goals. It's your job to help people see how their work on this plan will get them the things they want. You need to reach a win-win agreement with each employee that shows them all how they win when the company wins.

To do this successfully, you must think in a win-win fashion. *Win-win* means that your employees get something they want for the work they provide and the company gets what it wants because of their work. In this case the company's "wants" are the tasks from the team plan and goals. You need to work with the individuals on your team to help them define what they each want.

Remember that this is a win-win agreement, not a win–not-lose agreement. An agreement that says "Do these things and I won't fire you" is not motivating. That may work for low-skill occupations but not for complicated business processes. You want your employees to have a clear idea of what they are getting from the company for providing their services.

You want to take a win-win approach with your team. The people on your team want things from the company. Your employees will do the job based on their own motivations when they know they'll get what they want as a result. You will not have to nag them to get the job done. The hard part is helping people see what they really want.

Many employees will default to say that all they want is a paycheck. This is usually a cover for other motivations. People are rarely motivated by money—they are more likely to be demotivated by learning that someone else is making more than they are. Getting a paycheck rarely inspires people to do their best work. People need a deeper motivation for that.

Many people will be motivated by the opportunity to improve their skills or by the work itself. Other people may have skills or hobbies outside of work that the paycheck pays for. Others may like the recognition they get from doing the job well. Work with your employees individually to help them find their key.

Some employees will not share their real motivation with you. This is a personal question. In these cases, simply take them at face value that they are working for the paycheck and watch them. If they are good at what they do, you'll see other motivations coming through. If they are only mediocre, then perhaps they are only motivated by the paycheck.

CREATING A WIN-WIN AGREEMENT

Once you have a list of tasks the employee needs to perform and you have a clear idea of what your employee wants from the company, you are ready to record what both sides will do to create the results you want. Stephen Covey created an effective method for this known as the *win-win agreement*. He discusses it in detail in his book *First Things First*. This approach is a highly effective way to connect employees to their tasks.

The win-win agreement is the basis for proper delegation. Proper delegation occurs when the manager and the employee define the desired results and then the manager steps out of the way and lets the employee do the job. If the manager tries to tell the employee how to do the job, the manager is micromanaging and the employee will disengage from the work.

Of course, employees who are new to a role will need help and coaching so they can learn how to do the job. But in this case the manager is acting as a trainer, not a puppeteer. The goal is for the employee to take ownership of the project as soon as possible. This frees the manager to handle higher-value tasks.

Remember that win-win agreements are between the company and the employee—not between you and the employee. You are representing the interests of the company and offering resources from the company. This is an important distinction. Many managers make the mistake of getting caught in the middle between their employees and upper-level managers. You need to keep your independence and help your employees get what they want from the company and help the company get what it wants from the employees.

The win-win agreement has five parts:

- **Desired results.** This is a clear description of what the company and the employee want to have as a result of the agreement. The company wants the results and tasks to be completed. Employees may want many things. Money, training, and advancement are all possible desired results. Work with the employee to articulate the employee's desired results.
- **Resources.** These are the resources that the company and the employee will supply respectively to get the job done. Usually the employee is providing time—though in small companies the employee may provide some equipment or resources. The company may provide money, other people, or equipment. You can

also be a resource to the employee. You can define your training or coaching here.

- ✦ **Guidelines.** These are rules the employee has to follow when creating the desired results. They are also a place where you can communicate bad strategies to the employee. One obvious guideline is that the employee must follow the rules laid out in the company's ethics manual. A sample guideline might be "You cannot coach customers in how to answer the survey."

- ✦ **Measurement.** This is how the company and the employee will measure progress. Company results should be easy to define because they follow the SMART format discussed earlier. Measuring employee results might be more difficult. An employee might say she wants more responsibility. How would she measure that? By being clear here, you can provide the experience she expects rather than guessing. This is a good place to define how often you'll ask for status updates and what measurements you want to see.

- ✦ **Consequences.** This is where you'll describe the positive and negative consequences that come from achieving or not achieving the desired results. There are two kinds of consequences: natural consequences and created consequences. Natural consequences simply happen because of the results. For example, *If we don't achieve a rating of 90 percent "good" or "great" by our target date, at least 10 percent of our customers will see us as ineffective and we will lose sales.* Natural consequences also describe internal motivations. If you feel bad because you didn't do your best work, that is an internal motivation.

Created consequences are synthetic; that is, they are created by people. They are usually based on KITA management tools. For example, if we make our goals, we'll get a bonus; if we don't make our goals, we'll receive a low rating at review time. Synthetic consequences are usually not as motivating as intrinsic or natural consequences.

Here is an example of the win-win agreement I created with two employees to improve the reliability of a computer system:

- **Desired results.** I wanted the computer system to run more reliably. They wanted to receive a bonus.
- **Resources.** They could use allotted time during the workday, and the company would pay for any additional technical training they needed to solve the problems.
- **Guidelines.** The final system needed to send automatic reliability reports.
- **Measurement.** We used software to measure the percentage of jobs that the system completed successfully. This became our measure of success. The employees had one month to achieve a reliability of more than 90 percent.
- **Consequences.** If the employees solved the problem, they each got $1,000. If they didn't, we would suffer with unhappy customers and we'd keep having to put out fires.

This was a very successful arrangement. I had chosen employees with the talents to complete the job, and the promise of a spot bonus focused them on the task. In this case we used money to create the win-win agreement, but win-win rewards are limited only by your imagination.

Meet with each person on your team and create a win-win agreement so that you'll both be clear regarding expectations and contributions. Most companies have a formal review process that requires you to define goals and report on their accomplishment. You can use the work from the win-win agreement to fill these out easily.

COACHING
FOR SURVIVAL
AND GROWTH

While some layoffs affect entire departments or divisions, most layoff survivors are still employed because they are valuable to the company.

Some companies manage layoffs by making a prioritized list of people and drawing a line through the list. The key to layoff survival as a manager and team is to have team members in the top half of the list. You can create a team of high-performing individuals through coaching.

Coaching is a process by which you help each employee set professional goals and then make skill-based improvements. When you become good at coaching, you can make your people the best they can be and help them all avoid the layoff axe.

Here are your goals for the final week of this program:

COACH

DELIVERABLE	DESCRIPTION	DATE
Create coaching agreements with all willing team members.	Create coaching agreements so each of your people will have a clear development goal.	Week 12
Find a coaching moment.	Find an opportunity to coach your team members on a skill chosen in the coaching agreement.	Week 12
Deliver coaching feedback.	Deliver feedback to your employees to help them see behaviors and devise an improvement plan.	Week 12

Coaching is at the top of the management skills triangle because it is ineffective if you haven't built the whole foundation under it. If your team lacks trust, coaching won't work. If team members are not challenged, they won't care about growing. If your people are in the wrong jobs, no amount of coaching will save them; if they don't know what to do or why they're doing it, coaching will seem pointless.

Yet many managers make the mistake of trying to coach their teams without having built the necessary foundations. If you have followed all the steps in this plan, you will not have this problem. Now you just need to know how to coach. Coaching involves two aspects, covered in the next two chapters:

- Coaching to create a great team
- Coaching remote employees

When we coach, we find out what skills our people want to improve, and we help them by using our powers of observation to create a mirror for them. We explain what we see in them from the outside.

Once we have our coaching skills in place, we'll be able to take our motivated and directed staff and help them improve in the areas they want to improve or need to improve. Growing our people is the last step in our recovery process, and if we do our jobs right, it's where we get to spend most of our time.

13

COACHING TO CREATE
A GREAT TEAM

IMAGINE THE FOLLOWING scenario. You have a team of self-directed people who are committed to executing solid results and who have formed a plan to achieve them. These people are self-motivated and excited about their work. Each one of them knows what to do and when to do it, and if one of them gets into trouble, the others pitch in to help.

Why, then, would they need a manager? What's your job? You don't need to nag them, judge them, or direct them. It looks like you're out of work. This would be true if it weren't for coaching. A manager who achieves the ideal just described is left with the most fun part of the job—helping people achieve their personal goals and improve their skills.

When you become a great coach, people will fight to join your team. You'll get your pick of the best people in the company, and your team will have a reputation for excellence. And because of your coaching, your team will get better from year to year, outperforming the competition in the marketplace and creating a powerful cycle of improvement.

The approach we'll discuss is based on coaching methods developed at the Babson College coaching program and is described in more detail in *The Coaching Manager*, by James M. Hunt and Joseph R. Weintraub.

Tiger Woods is the best golfer in the world. Yet he pays lots of money for a personal coach. It's obvious that the coach is not a better golfer than Tiger. So what does the coach do for him? He does what all great coaches do. He helps Tiger see himself.

A coach is a highly skilled mirror. Tiger needs a coach because he cannot watch himself swing. Even if he watched himself on videotape, it would be difficult for him to judge his swing objectively. A coach provides the intelligent mirror Tiger needs. The most effective coaches simply point out the problem areas. Someone who sees a problem area clearly can usually correct it with a little guidance.

As a coach, you hold a mirror up to your employees to help them improve the skills they want or need to improve the most. The following steps help you do this effectively:

FOCUS ON YOUR BEST PLAYERS

Let's do a thought experiment. Imagine that you have three piles of money in front of you. One pile has $10, another has $20, and a third pile has $50. You can take all the money after you make this decision.

I will allow you to multiply one of these piles by three. You can pick any pile, multiply it by three, and take all three piles of money. This is not a trick question. Which pile do you multiply by three? I hope that you chose to multiply the $50 pile. That would have given you $180 total.

Time for the same thought experiment. Imagine that you have three employees on your team. One is barely making it and is having trouble keeping up with the team. One is an average player and does what is asked. The third is a star who accomplishes every task easily and shows drive and initiative.

Which employee's productivity do you choose to multiply with your attention? I hope you said you would multiply the star and perhaps create a superstar. Focusing our coaching on a star dramatically increases that star's productivity and makes your team stronger.

Sadly, most managers don't follow this strategy. Instead they focus their attention on their weakest players. They try to bring subpar people up to average. This makes as much sense as multiplying the $10 pile. There is no way to make a subpar player into a star. You're much better off making a star into a superstar.

1. Create a coaching environment.
2. Agree on coaching goals.
3. Capture a coaching moment.
4. Observe objectively.
5. Share observations.
6. Make a plan for improvement.
7. Look for the next coaching moment.

In sporting events, these practices are easy. The players want to be coached, and the practices and games present obvious coaching moments. The coach will give the feedback, sometimes immediately, and the player will repeat the action and incorporate the feedback.

In the business world it takes a little more effort to set up the coaching process. Let's look at each of the seven steps in detail.

Taking the First Step to Great Coaching

The first thing you need is an environment where coaching can work. Employees who accept coaching are putting themselves in a vulnerable position. They have to come to you and admit their weaknesses and ask for help. This is hard for anyone to do, but it can be particularly hard to do with a boss.

Employees don't like to admit weaknesses to their bosses, and right after a layoff there is even less incentive to do so. This is why coaching requires the collaborative environment you've been building. The employees need to see that they will improve their position by choosing areas to work on and getting your help.

This brings up a dilemma that exists for all managers. How do you balance the trust that goes into being a coach with the judgment that goes into being a manager? Your company wants you to create a high-performing team—doing that requires trust. Your company also wants you to rank people for raises and layoffs—doing that hurts trust. How can you balance that?

Like all dilemmas, this one has no solution. The best you can do is to recognize the situation and manage it. You need to teach people to think of jobs as opportunities to improve their skills. Therefore, coaching is helpful even if the employees must admit some weaknesses to someone who needs to judge their performance. Employees must understand the following:

➤ **Performance issues cannot be hidden forever.** After a while, everyone in a group knows who is strong and who needs help in certain areas. An employee who avoids improving so as to hide a weakness will not be around for long.

➤ **Performance improvement is the best job security.** Employees who engage in the coaching process will develop better skills and will be more valuable.

➤ **Employees need to look beyond this job.** Employees need to have the foresight to start thinking about future jobs. Employees who participate in coaching are improving their chances of having a successful career.

➤ **You are there for them.** This is a key piece of the coaching process. Your employees need to believe that you have their best interests at heart when you coach them. They must not think that your notes are going on their permanent record to be used against them. A manager who can create an environment where employees feel safe to ask for coaching has done great work. This is the first step toward making your team members the strongest people in the company. This is a sure antidote to layoffs.

DEVELOP COACHING AGREEMENTS

There is an old joke that asks the question "How many psychiatrists does it take to change a lightbulb?" The answer is, "One, but it really has to want to change." The same is true of coaching. You'll have successful coaching sessions only with someone who wants to improve. You ensure this by mutually agreeing to coaching goals.

There are two reasons that it is essential for you and the employee to agree on the area where the employee wants to improve:

MAKE A CRITICALITY LIST

Make a criticality list by asking yourself, "If I had to cut someone from the team, whose absence would have the least impact?" Write that person's name down and then look at the remaining list of people and ask the question again. Keep asking the question until you get to the top.

You are probably asking yourself, "What kind of cruel new trick is this? I just had a layoff. Why do I need another life-boat list?" The answer is that we always need to have a current criticality list for our team members. This is essential to coaching.

I once had to do a criticality list as part of an employee review process. We blended my team with another team to make the list; then we used this list to apportion raises. When we were done with the process, a guy on my team, Lance, was at the bottom.

This was not Lance's fault. Lance was a smart, hardworking guy. He implemented well, and he had a great personality. Lance wound up at the bottom of the list because he was focused on products that were not important to our company. He was expendable because of his assignment.

When the ranking was over, I asked Lance to meet with me. I told him that he was at the bottom of the criticality list. Understandably, he was shocked and angry. Then I told him that we were going to fix the problem. We put a training program in place to give Lance skills with our flagship product. I got him assignments that focused him on that product, and he developed skills and a reputation that moved him from the bottom of the list.

Lance went on to have a successful career because he and I had used the data from the criticality list to create a coaching moment. The criticality list highlighted data that was important to both of us.

You need to understand which team members need coaching and where they need to go. Creating a criticality list will give you the insight necessary to become a great coach.

- **People change only when they are self-motivated.** As in the lightbulb joke, people work on change only if they see it is necessary. You cannot teach someone who sees no reason to learn or who isn't interested.
- **Focusing on everything is the same as focusing on nothing.** To coach successfully, you need to capture moments when an employee is trying a new skill and use those for coaching. You can succeed in doing this only if you are looking at one specific skill for a period of time. When you and the employee agree on what needs to be improved, your data gathering and your conversations become focused.

There may be cases in which the employee wants to target something that is a relatively low priority. While you may suggest other options, you cannot force someone to learn. It's possible that the person's highest-priority area is also an area of great vulnerability and sensitivity. When you start with something that is safe for the person, you build trust to work on higher-priority items.

When you choose a coaching topic, clearly define the area of concern and how you and the employee would measure success. This gives you a target to shoot for and allows you to declare victory and move on to a new area.

CAPTURING COACHING MOMENTS

Once you've created a goal with your employee, you need to be alert for coaching moments. These are natural times during the day when the person is attempting to use the skills being coached. For example, say that Katherine wants to improve her persuasion skills. You are in a meeting with Katherine, and you see that she is trying to get the team to adopt her plan to meet one of the project requirements. You note that Katherine is not listening to her counterparts and is simply waiting for her turn to talk. Predictably, her attempts at influence fail.

This is a coaching moment. While this is happening, you should begin making observations about how Katherine is approaching the encounter. After the meeting, you invite Katherine to meet with you because you have some feedback that may help her quest to become more persuasive.

Your up-front agreement with Katherine to help her improve her communication skills makes the coaching much more effective. You knew that Katherine wanted to improve her persuasiveness, so you were alert to the situation. When you suggest a meeting, Katherine is open to the meeting because she asked for your help in this area.

This is much better than the random coaching one usually sees in the workplace: "Katherine, do you have a minute? I have some feedback for you." In those cases a manager has randomly noted something that needs improving and wants to bring it to the person's attention. However, without previous buy-in, this meeting becomes more of a reprimand than a coaching session. It's the reason that *feedback* has become a dirty word.

GIVING EFFECTIVE FEEDBACK

This is the most difficult task of good coaching. A good coach holds up a mirror to people and helps them see themselves objectively. When the coach does this well, people see their own mistakes and fix them. The problem in coaching is that the manager's own inferences and judgments distort the mirror.

Consider the case of Katherine. The manager might be tempted to say to Katherine, "Katherine, I noticed that you were trying to persuade Joel to follow your approach. You didn't listen to him when he spoke to you. Because you weren't listening, he wasn't listening, and you just made him angry instead of persuading him."

This seems like a fairly benign description of what happened. But in this case the manager has distorted the mirror with inferences. Katherine may become defensive at this point. She may claim that she was listening and that Joel just hates her anyway. She may claim that the manager always sides with Joel. Once Katherine has become defensive, the coaching moment is over.

When you are watching people attempting new skills, you need to be clear about the differences between observations and inferences. Observations are objective facts that someone else could see on a videotape and verify.

If a videotape would have shown Katherine speaking immediately after Joel, and neglecting to paraphrase his point, then your feedback that she spoke without paraphrasing would be an observation. But the assertion that Katherine wasn't listening cannot be seen on a videotape, so this assertion is an inference.

You need to clearly separate your observations from your inferences when you make coaching observations. A good way to do this is to create a T-shaped form in your notebook.

This diagram gives you a simple way to capture what you've seen and what you inferred it to mean. In Katherine's case you'd have something like Figure 13.1.

These notes are there just to help you in your coaching conversation with Katherine. It's best if you informally write them in your notebook rather than on an official form. This helps avoid concerns that you may be "gathering ammunition."

Remember the two key points of great coaching:

✦ You are acting as a mirror for the person you are coaching.
✦ The person being coached is internally motivated to improve.

Given these conditions, you can use a light touch when you are coaching. In the best of all worlds, the coach will make the observations, interpret them, and provide the next steps. Often the person will take a hint from the fact that you asked to meet and will search his or her memory of the situation for areas to improve.

Try starting a coaching session with the question like "How did it go?" This lets the coachee take the lead. In cases where the coachee can't see the situation, you should share your observations and see if the person can jump to your inferences. For example,

FIGURE 13.1

FORM FOR RECORDING OBSERVATIONS VS. INFERENCES

Observations	Inferences
Katherine spoke immediately after Joel	Katherine was not listening to Joel
Katherine did not paraphrase Joel's words	
Joel crossed his arms and looked out the window	Joel was angry and remained unconvinced

with Katherine you might say, "I noticed that when you were talking to Joel you waited until he finished speaking and then said your piece without paraphrasing his point of view." That might be enough for Katherine to say, "You're right. I guess I wasn't listening. I would have persuaded him better if he had felt heard." Since you have Katherine's agreement that she wants to improve her persuasion skills, she is likely to try to figure out what happened on her own.

In cases where the person does not see what you saw and does not grasp the interpretation, you will want to share your observations and inferences. So if Katherine didn't understand your point, you could say, "Since you didn't paraphrase what Joel said, I took it to mean that you weren't listening. I suspect Joel may have taken it that way as well." This may cause Katherine to think through the next step.

Neutral observation of facts is the safest way to provide corrective feedback. Let's say you asked John for a report by Friday. When you don't have the report on Monday morning, you should say, "John, I asked for that report on Friday, but I don't see it." This provides room for John to correct himself or give the reason. You are just stating the facts.

It also protects you in case you made an error. For example, if John had put the report on your desk, where it got covered, he can respond with "That's strange. I put it on your desk." And you can go find it without being embarrassed.

Imagine what would have happened if you had said, "I asked you for that report by last Friday, and you missed the deadline," and it turns out the report was on your desk. Now John is likely to be insulted, and if you made the mistake, you'll have some work to do to fix the relationship.

Your goal in sharing your observations is to hold the mirror up to the coachee and let the coachee draw the lessons from it. Coachees draw these lessons faster as they learn the skills being taught. Once they understand the skills, coachees will often create their own correction plan as soon as they see the problem.

HELPING PEOPLE HELP THEMSELVES

Now that you both understand what happened at that last coaching moment, it's time to plan improvement for the next one. It is best if the coachee develops the improvement plan because it ensures buy-in. When you tell the coachee what to do, you take ownership away from the employee.

Questions are your most powerful coaching tool. Ask open-ended questions that encourage the coachees to think through the problem. For example, you might ask Katherine, "What do you think you could have done differently to influence Joel?" This might cause her to describe the problem and what she will do next time to fix it.

EXERT YOUR INFLUENCE

When you come into the office a little late, they are watching. When you lose your temper, they are watching. When you bitch about your boss, they are watching. And they will repeat everything you do. Whatever you do, that's what you'll get.

You are a manager, and so you have profound influence over your people, whether you want it or not. Two words describe your influence: *powerful* and *subtle*. Folks may not admit that they watch you or that they emulate you, but they do.

This means that if you want your people to arrive early, you should arrive early. If you want them to be polite, you should be polite. If you want them to be happy, you should be happy. Whatever you do, as subtle as it is, they will pick up on it and they will follow it.

I remember one manager who had a positive influence on me because of his behavior outside work. He was a cyclist. And not just any cyclist—a really fast cyclist with a fantastic bike.

Wouldn't you know that after working for him for only a few months I bought a bike? I didn't become a world-class cyclist, but I rode quite a bit. Seeing him cycling got me noticing cyclists as I drove home. Then conversations about bikes got me thinking about what bike I would own. Then conversations about cycling to work got me to thinking about whether that was possible.

Then I bought a bike.

You can do the same for your team. Be a positive influence on your team. Become the change you want to create, and your team will follow you without even knowing it.

Occasionally you may want to give the person some knowledge to help him or her think through the problem. In Katherine's case you might say, "Katherine, people tend to be influenced by people they feel they can influence. Do you think Joel feels he can influence you? How might you change that?"

The plan you come up with should describe specific behaviors that the coachee will modify at the next opportunity. They should be things that you could observe objectively.

You now need to keep watch for the next time the person uses the skills and repeat your observation process. Be sure to recognize when someone is attempting to implement the plan you made together and encourage successes. If the person has trouble, then record your observations and share them so that the coachee can try again.

COACHING REMOTE EMPLOYEES

COACHING AN EMPLOYEE remotely is like trying to help someone choose a tie over the phone. It's very difficult because the process of coaching is inherently one of observation. As coaches, we look for a coaching moment, make observations, and then share our observations with our coachee. We avoid inferences, or at least we specify them as our inferences during our feedback sessions.

This is much more difficult with a remote employee. We cannot see our remote employee, so it is difficult to catch spontaneous coaching moments. Our communication bandwidth is limited, so we can't tell exactly what's going on for the coachee. These limitations make it difficult, but not impossible, to give good coaching. We simply have to focus our attention on the things we can do.

COACHING VISITS

Remember the seagull manager, who flies in, craps all over everything, and flies away? The seagull manager is a lousy coach, and that seagull visit is not a coaching visit.

221

A coaching visit is an agreed-upon visit where you have scheduled a coaching moment with one of your team members. For example, I live in the Boston area, and I once had an employee who lived in Arizona. We agreed to meet in Texas where he was giving a presentation, because I had agreed to coach him on his presentation skills.

This is a coaching visit. I watched my team member present as part of an existing coaching agreement. I knew what skills the team member wanted to improve, and when I arrived and watched him present, he felt that I was providing a service, not rendering a judgment. We both wished that I had more opportunities to work with him and that we could see more of each other.

This never happens when a seagull comes to visit.

Coaching Nonvisual Skills

If you don't have an opportunity to coach your team member through in-person visits, you could focus your energies on nonvisual skills. For example, running a teleconference meeting is a challenging skill that is perfect for long-distance coaching. By sitting in the audience like anyone else on the call, you can make direct observations about what the meeting was like for you. Did it go past its scheduled ending time? Did you get lost regarding the topic? Were you unable to read the slides on the desktop sharing software? All these observations are fair points for coaching and offer opportunities for valuable feedback for your remote team member.

Use One-on-One Telephone Time to Help Your Team Member Self-Coach

The best coaching happens when you're in the room, making independent observations as your coachee works. This way you can hold a mirror up to the employee and provide an outside perspective.

KNOW THE THREE KEYS TO GREAT PERFORMANCE

There are three qualities we can bring to our teams as managers that will create fantastic results. Each of these three qualities is excellent in its own right, but when combined they produce great-performing employees.

1. **Expect greatness.** People will give you what you expect of them. If you expect them to have problems, to squabble, or to be depressed, you'll get that. But if you expect them to pull together, do a great job, and be one of the best groups in the team, you'll get greatness.

   Have great expectations for your team and it will change the way you think and the questions you ask of yourself. Instead of asking "How can I get these people to do what it takes?" you'll ask "How can we be as great as we should?" and that will give you better answers.

2. **Always be respectful.** Always remember that the people on your team are trying to do the best they can and deserve your respect. Always treat them with courtesy and as professionals and they will reward you by treating you with courtesy, even if they don't agree with you.

3. **Teach people.** Part of expecting greatness is expecting your team members to learn and grow. Part of respecting them is assuming they have the capacity to learn and grow. If you expect your people to be great, and you respect them, all you have to do is teach them. Take the time to coach them and help them build the skills they need to meet your high expectations.

That's it. When you combine high expectations with respect and teaching, you've got all the ingredients you need for a high-performing team.

You can also help your employees learn to act as their own mirrors. Say you have an employee who wants to improve influence skills in working with outside companies. When that employee visits a partner, you'd have a coaching moment, if you could be there. Since you can't, you need to do the second-best thing: let the coachee describe the meeting over the phone.

Start your phone call by asking your coachee to describe the meeting in detail. You don't have to say anything at this point; just let the coachee describe what happened. This will force your coachee to review the meeting to tell the story.

Then ask your coachee questions about the meeting: "How do you think it went?" "What would you have liked to have done

223

differently?" and then just listen. A motivated coachee will be able to analyze the meeting, develop some personal observations, and create an action plan for the next meeting.

You can combine this approach with coaching visits. Perhaps after several meetings you'll have a chance to visit with your coachee. Then that coaching visit would fit right in with the process you've been following over the phone.

CREATE SCORECARDS

What gets measured gets done, but who knows what's being measured if nobody keeps score? Creating scorecards is an excellent way to focus your team on what's important and to give the team goals to improve upon. It's also an invaluable tool for working with remote teams. Scorecards can go on Web pages and be updated automatically to provide constant feedback to anyone on the team at any time of day.

When I managed a customer support team, we wanted to make sure that when customers called they talked to a live person rather than voice mail. So we measured the percentage of calls that were picked up live, and I posted that information on the wall in a graph. I also had individual graphs for each person, which I handed out privately. We routinely answered over 90 percent of our calls with a live person because this is what we were measuring.

There are three steps to creating scorecards that work:

1. **Pick an easily quantifiable statistic as something that is important to your team.** Sales teams have always had it easy in this regard—they count money. Other teams can do the same thing. Engineering teams can count the number of times they hit milestones on time. Marketing teams can measure product sales or the number of tools they give to the sales force. Whatever statistic you pick, make sure it is easily measurable.

    Beware of a statistic that can be manipulated. For example, if your software team is measuring the number of bugs in the software, make sure that folks continue to put bugs into the system

CREATE HALLWAY CONVERSATIONS

f your team is spread across a continent or across the world, use instant messaging to create the effect of hallway conversations.

Collocated teams have an advantage over distributed teams. They can have impromptu conversations when two folks go to get a cup of coffee. They'll be standing there, waiting for the coffee machine to dispense its precious brew, when Mary will turn to Sal and ask, "Hey, did you ever hear from that guy in marketing?"

"No," says Sal. "You're right—I never heard from that guy. I'll give him a call."

Sal calls the guy in marketing, and the team saves a week because the guy had forgotten the request.

Hallway conversations are subtle but valuable tools. Replacing them on your distributed team will help tremendously.

You can re-create some of the magic of the hallway with instant-messaging systems. Almost everyone has an instant messenger account today, so ask your team to publish them. It's likely that not everyone will be on the same system (Google Talk, Yahoo, AIM, etc.), but you can work around that problem.

All you have to do is join the same services as the folks on your team, and then use a website or software client that lets you see all of them in one place. (These are often called multi-platform chat clients.) You'll be able to see when folks log in and give them a "Good morning" just as if you were walking by their desks. If you show your team how to use the aggregator, you can have a fully connected distributed team, and Mary can now IM Sal to say, "Hey, did you ever hear from that guy in marketing?"

when they are found. There is nothing worse than having a team manipulate its measurement systems just to fool itself (or you).

2. **Consistently gather the data on that statistic.** Make sure you're willing to follow through and gather the data before you choose to implement a scorecard. There are few things as demoralizing as initiatives that sputter and die due to lack of manager interest. Once you start gathering data, gather it regularly. Make it part of the fabric of the team.

3. **Publish the data.** You can publish the data privately to your team in an e-mail or publicly by posting it on the wall. I did both with my team. Be sure to publish it in some way, though, because failure to follow through on this step will damage your credibility in the eyes of your team.

Creating a scorecard for your team requires imagination and discipline. Like all things that require imagination and discipline, it rewards those who follow through. In the case of your team, it will keep folks focused on what is important.

LOOK FOR CRITICAL SKILLS

To focus on what is important, your remote employees (as well as your on-site team members) need to excel at the skills required to do their specific jobs. All tasks have five or six critical skills that

PROVIDE DATA FOR YOUR TEAM MEMBER'S RÉSUMÉ

If we are going to make a new kind of deal with our employees that trades loyalty for the new form of job security, we need to walk the talk. We need to help our team members write their résumés.

I'm not talking about wordsmithing the résumés with them or crafting job descriptions. I'm talking about providing your team with the data they need for a great résumé. Ironically, focusing on these data reduces the chances that they will ever need the data.

Great résumés contain data that relate directly to revenue. A résumé entry that says "Led a cross-functional team" stinks of bureaucracy and a lack of measurable results. A résumé entry that says "Drove customer satisfaction from 80 percent to 95 percent by leading a cross-functional team" catches the reader's attention and gets the interview.

Do you have numbers like this for your team? Can you point to specific, measurable numbers that tell a story of revenue generation or customer satisfaction? Can you point to your product's market size or the size of your customer base? Can you point to surveys that say you are doing a good job? If not, are you serving your team?

Help your team members write great résumés by finding ways to connect their activities to measurable customer results. This has three benefits:

+ Team members get the data they need to value their career.
+ The team's motivation increases, because they see how they are affecting your company's results.
+ You have the data you need to keep further layoffs from affecting your team.

By helping your team see their solid connection to the big picture, you are walking the walk about trading loyalty for the new form of job security.

control how well someone can do a job. What are the skills? They're different for all jobs, but they always exist. Before you can coach your team members, you need to figure out the five or six critical skills for the job.

Figuring out the five or six skills requires some thought. They need to be skills that are independent of each other. You can't say that one skill is "good communication skills" and another skill is "excellent presentations." One of these skills assumes the other. You want your five or six skills to be set up so that a team member can be great at one skill and terrible at another. Here's an example of five skills for a technical sales engineer:

- **Technical strength.** The sales engineer must understand the technology.
- **Presentation skills.** The sales engineer must be able to demo and present well.
- **Time management.** These folks get pulled in many directions and need to be able to manage multiple priorities.
- **Rapport building.** As a sales engineer, you need to be able to enter a company and quickly make friends with your customers.
- **Sales savvy.** A sales engineer must understand what's happening in a sales situation and follow the account manager's lead.

Once you have these five skills identified, you can start improving your team. You can measure each member on the five skills and use the skills as the basis of annual reviews and coaching sessions. You can use them to help your team members identify areas of growth and create coaching opportunities.

Don't worry if your company has already defined competencies for your team's reviews. If you've done your job right with the skills, it will be easy to map skills to competencies, and you can still use the skills to manage.

Coaching is a gift that all great managers give to their employees. Find a way to give this gift to everyone on your team, and you'll be rewarded with a team that consistently grows toward being one of the best in the company.

In Closing

WHEN YOU PICK up a business magazine, you're likely to see a picture of a CEO on the cover. These magazine covers give the impression that the CEOs of companies are the most important people in business. Is it true?

Business magazines, shareholders, and board members would say yes. They would point out that a great CEO can make a mediocre company take off. They know that the CEO is the one person whose influence spans the organization. Great CEOs can singlehandedly create great companies—just look at Steve Jobs and his turnaround at Apple.

Yet if you ask individual contributors to name the most important person in the company, they are likely to say, "My boss." Their boss is their frontline manager. That means you.

Our immediate bosses have more influence over whether we have a good day than anyone else. People join companies because of the company's future, products, or vision. They stay based on how much they like their immediate supervisor. As a manager, you have more influence than anyone else in the company over whether the people on your team are motivated and productive or unmotivated and listless.

There is a lot of pressure on you. Very few people like the idea of playing God, and those who do rarely make good managers. You probably didn't become a manager so you could be the single largest influence in someone's work life, but there you have it—you are.

This is why it's great to see that you made it all the way through this book. Great managers are not born; they are made. And they are made through a consistent pattern of personal growth and learning. Great managers read about management, and they think about their actions. They know that sometimes the instinctual thing to do is not the best thing to do, and they consider how their actions will affect the lives of the people on their teams and those around them.

Your company's management implemented a layoff because the managers believed it was the best way to thrive and grow in the future. They chose to keep you on after the layoff because they believed you were the best choice available to help make their dream of a stronger company a reality.

Your managers have handed you a difficult job. Layoffs destroy the fabric of teamwork. They disrupt life, depress your team, and threaten to make every day at work a day of drudgery. They sap the energy from an organization, damaging our confidence that we can achieve our goals as a company and as individuals. Layoffs show us just how much of our work lives is out of our control.

Many managers fall by the wayside at this point, acknowledging to themselves that they were never cut out for leadership, that they don't want all that pressure, that they would prefer to go back to being an individual contributor where they have to worry about only their own work and have only one boss. I suspect, though, that you are not one of these folks. After all, those folks never reach a chapter called "In Closing" when they read a management book.

Instead, I think you are someone who sees your role as a manager as an opportunity to make your company a better place to work. I think you're somebody who wants the ball when the game is on the line and you believe you can make a difference in people's lives. I believe you're ready to ignore things that are out of your control and focus on the things you can control: your relationship with your team members and your ability to help them make a plan for the future. You're ready to focus on the five key management skills.

You used five skills to recover from this layoff: collaborate, challenge, choose, connect, and coach. By now you've seen that these are not only skills for hard times but skills for good times as well. They are timeless, and they always have value.

You may have learned these skills during hard times, because hard times are when we need to get down to fundamentals. In good times it's easy to ignore problems. The lack of collaboration on your team isn't hurting anyone. After all, everybody is getting bonuses, and you're a hero. As John Madden, the football coach, said, "Winning covers a lot of stink."

During these hard times you have an opportunity to do something rare. You have a chance to build a team from the ground up. To create a strong foundation built upon strong relationships and a shared mission. You can create a team that is a shining example of energy in a company where everybody spends the day waiting for the other shoe to drop.

Best of all, you can create a place where your employees love to work. You can create a daily environment where the people you work with enjoy themselves because they know they're accomplishing something together. You can make a team where you and your team members will be happy.

After all, that's what great managers do.

Additional Resources:
Great Books to Help You Succeed

Becoming a Successful Manager: How to Make a Smooth Transition from Managing Yourself to Managing Others, by Jack Grossman (McGraw-Hill, 2001). This is the best book I've found to help a new manager get started.

The Coaching Manager, by James M. Hunt and Joseph R. Weintraub (Sage, 2002). With strong cases and examples, this book digs deeply into what it takes to be a great coach.

First, Break All the Rules, by Marcus Buckingham and Curt Coffman (Simon & Schuster, 1999). Being a great manager requires different strategies than you'd expect. This book shatters some common myths.

First Things First, by Stephen R. Covey, A. Roger Merrill, and Rebecca R. Merrill (Free Press, 2001). The *7 Habits* book introduced the win-win agreement. *First Things First* perfects the explanation.

Healing the Downsized Organization, by Delorese Ambrose (Random House, 1997). Shows how to help your team through the trauma of a layoff.

Healing the Wounds, by David M. Noer (Jossey-Bass, 1995). Identifies the syndrome of "layoff survivor sickness" and how to combat it.

Influence Without Authority, by Allan R. Cohen and David L. Bradford (Wiley & Sons, 1991). A handbook on office politics and how to master external collaboration.

Now, Discover Your Strengths, by Marcus Buckingham and Donald O. Clifton (Free Press, 2001). Takes the topic of talents and strengths to the next level. Links to an online test that helps you discover your strengths.

On Becoming a Leader, by Warren Bennis (Perseus, 2003). Teaches the reasons behind becoming a leader and what it takes to succeed in that role.

The One Page Business Plan, by Jim Horan (One Page Business Plan, 1998). Shows you how to capture the team's challenge and planning on one page. Also has some great exercises.

Power Up!, by Allan R. Cohen and David L. Bradford (Wiley & Sons, 1998). A complete overview of collaborative leadership.

The 7 Habits of Highly Effective People, by Stephen R. Covey (Simon & Schuster, 2004). This book is applicable to every aspect of leading. It is a classic with basic principles you need to succeed in management.

Index